THE BEST ENTERPRISE RISK MANAGEMENT
AIRLINE AND AIRPORT BUSINESS

Ayse KUCUK YILMAZ

THE BEST ENTERPRISE RISK MANAGEMENT PRACTICE FOR AIRLINE AND AIRPORT BUSINESS

Business Management and a New Managerial Approach for Corporate Sustainability

VDM Verlag Dr. Müller

Imprint

Bibliographic information by the German National Library: The German National Library lists this publication at the German National Bibliography; detailed bibliographic information is available on the Internet at http://dnb.d-nb.de.

Any brand names and product names mentioned in this book are subject to trademark, brand or patent protection and are trademarks or registered trademarks of their respective holders. The use of brand names, product names, common names, trade names, product descriptions etc. even without a particular marking in this works is in no way to be construed to mean that such names may be regarded as unrestricted in respect of trademark and brand protection legislation and could thus be used by anyone.

Cover image: www.purestockx.com

Publisher:
VDM Verlag Dr. Müller Aktiengesellschaft & Co. KG , Dudweiler Landstr. 125 a, 66123 Saarbrücken, Germany,
Phone +49 681 9100-698, Fax +49 681 9100-988,
Email: info@vdm-verlag.de

Zugl.: Eskisehir, Anadolu University, Social Science Institue Civil Aviation Management Department, Diss., 2007

Copyright © 2008 VDM Verlag Dr. Müller Aktiengesellschaft & Co. KG and licensors
All rights reserved. Saarbrücken 2008

Produced in USA and UK by:
Lightning Source Inc., La Vergne, Tennessee, USA
Lightning Source UK Ltd., Milton Keynes, UK
BookSurge LLC, 5341 Dorchester Road, Suite 16, North Charleston, SC 29418, USA

ISBN: 978-3-8364-6789-6

HE9780 .K84 2008
0134 111 030 182
Kucuk Yilmaz, Ayse.

The best enterprise risk
 management practice for
      2008.

2008 09 04

TABLE OF CONTENTS

PREFACE 5

DEDICATION 13

CHAPTERS

CHAPTER I

ONE SIZE DOES NOT FIT ALL: SHAPING OF THE ENTERPRISE RISK MANAGEMENT FRAMEWORKS

1. INTRODUCTION 15
2. BENEFITS OF ENTERPRISE RISK MANAGEMENT 22
3. IMPORTANCE OF ENTERPRISE RISK MANAGEMENT 24
4. LIMITATIONS OF ENTERPRISE RISK MANAGEMENT 30

CHAPTER II

THE ENTERPRISE RISK MANAGEMENT FRAMEWORKS

1. INTRODUCTION 32
2. SAMPLES FOR THE ENTERPRISE RISK MANAGEMENT FRAMEWORKS 36
    - 2.1. The Combined Code and Turnbull Guidance 37
    - 2.2. King II Report 38
    - 2.3. A Risk Management Standard by the Federation of European Risk Management Association (FERMA) 39
    - 2.4. Australian/New Zealand Standard 4360—Risk Management 39
    - 2.5. COSO's Enterprise Risk Management—Integrated Framework 41

2.6. The Institute of Management Accountants' (IMA) "A Global Perspective on Assessing Internal Control over Financial Reporting" (ICoFR)   48
2.7. Basel II   49
2.8. Standard & Poor's and Enterprise Risk Management   50
2.9. Risk and Insurance Management Society (RIMS) Risk Maturity Model   50
2.10. AIRMIC   52
2.11. An Overview Comparison of the AIRMIC /ALARM/IRM Risk Management Standard with: the Australia/New Zealand Standard AS/NZS 4360:2004   54
2.12. Transport Canada   64
2.13. Japaneese Industrial Risk Management Standard   67
2.14. British Standard   68
2.15. FAA Safety Risk Management   70

3. INTEGRATING ENTERPRISE RISK MANAGEMENT INTO THE ONGOING MANAGEMENT ACTIVITIES   72

CHAPTER III

BEST PRACTICES CONCEPT IN THE ENTERPRISE RISK MANAGEMENT

1. BEST PRACTICE DEFINITION   76
2. BEST PRACTICE FRAMEWORKS   77
3. KEY CONCLUSIONS   90

CHAPTER IV

THE BEST ENTERPRISE RISK MANAGEMENT PRACTICE IN AIR TRANSPORTATION SECTOR: AIRLINE AND AIRPORT BUSINESS

1. INTRODUCTION   94
2. THE AIRLINE RISK MANAGEMENT SURVEY   98

3. BEST PRACTICE SAMPLES TO ENTERPRISE RISK MANAGEMENT: AIRLINE BUSINESS 108

    3.1. LUFTHANSA 108
    3.2. CONTINENTAL AIRLINES 123
    3.3. DELTA AIRLINES 128
    3.4. FINNAIR 131
    3.5. AUSTRIAN AIRLINE 138
    3.6. SILVERJET 139
    3.7. JETBLUE 153

CHAPTER V

THE BEST ENTERPRISE RISK MANAGEMENT OPERATOR FOR AIRPORT BUSINESS

1. INTRODUCTION 177
2. THE ENTERPRISE RISK MANAGEMENT TO AIRPORT BUSINESS 182
3. CONCEPT OF ENTERPRISE RISK MANAGEMENT AND BEST PRACTICE 184
    3.1. Best Practice Concept to ERM and ERM Framework 187
    3.2. Best Practice Framework to ERM 188
4. DETERMINING OF BEST PRACTICE CRITERIA TO ENTERPRISE RISK MANAGEMENT 189
5. THE CURRENT ENTERPRISE RISK MANAGEMENT PRACTICES IN AIRPORT BUSINESS: FRAPORT A.G. AND TAV AIRPORT HOLDING CO. 191
    5.1. ERM Practice in FRAPORT AG 192
    5.2. ERM Practice in TAV Airportt Holding Co. 206
6. APPLICATION OF PROPOSED ANP MODEL TO THE BEST ERM PRACTICE 209
7. CONCLUSION OF THE CHAPTER 216

FINAL REMARKS ABOUT THE BOOK 219
REFERENCES 221

PREFACE

Risk is a fundamental and inseparable aspect of business. Providing maximum shareholder value is possible if enterprise-wide risks are effectively and truly managed. Confronting opportunities includes many risks. Therefore, determining, measuring, and managing corporate risks are the most important factors for the achievement of sustainable development objectives in business management. Today's airport and airline business is under pressure as a result of the development of the international markets, globalization, liberalization, commercialization, privatization, expectation of raised effectiveness and cost reduction, hardly legal regulations, rapid technological developments, and increasing competition. The cost of making mistakes is increasing day by day. The possibility of compensation to the faults is gradually reducing. The risk-profit balance should be established by managers. It has been shown that earning should be optimized by increasing output and decreasing operational costs and loss.

In today's business environment, Enterprise Risk Management is a necessity; it is not an option for the airport and airline managers in the air transportation industry. Enterprise Risk Management is increasing corporate value by providing sustainable competitive advantages and cost optimization, increasing business performance, and focusing all value sources on the company. Enterprise Risk Management presents many valuable benefits to business managers. To take advantage of these benefits, Enterprise Risk Management framework models should be developed and tailored to each company.

The book prepared to provide some insight on the challenges and rewards of "best-practice" enterprise risk management including enterprise risk management frameworks, implementation criteria, methodologies and processes. The aim of this book is to explain enterprise risk management frameworks and the characteristics of the best Enterprise Risk Management practices, and to provide the fundamental requirements for the best Enterprise Risk Management implementation. Another aim of the book is the presentation of a new approach to selecting the best operator for Enterprise Risk Management implementation in the air transportation industry.

Enterprise Risk Management provides a company with the process it needs to become more anticipatory and effective at evaluating, embracing and managing the uncertainties it faces as it creates sustainable value for stakeholders. It helps an organization manage its risks to protect and enhance enterprise value in three ways. First, it helps to establish sustainable competitive advantage. Second, it optimizes the cost of managing risk. Third, it helps management improve business performance (DeLoach, 2005).

Enterprise Risk Management has the potential to be in the highly competitive business environment for managers as a most important managerial approach and system. However, awareness should be raised about Enterprise Risk Management in the business world regarding the driving of this potential. Therefore, first, an explanation of the Enterprise Risk Management framework concept and an understanding of the implementation criteria of the best Enterprise Risk Management practice are essential and is the most important subject. Managing all enterprise risks is the most important element to achieving sustainable growth targets. This hypothesis should be understood by business managers. The well established Enterprise risk Management framework and its system are flexible to respond to change, and it should be tailored to an organization's corporate strategies, corporate objectivec, business activities, and external environment. In addition, an effective Enterprise Risk Management requires strong board and senior management oversight and support.

Dr. Ayse KUCUK YILMAZ

Managing of all enterprise risks are most important element to the achieving of the sustainable growth's targets. This conjecture should be well understood by managers. Managers should not have the expectation of providing all benefits of Enterprise Risk Management as always, one-to-one, and in the short-term. Enterprise Risk Management is a managerial style that should permeate every cell of the organization. Benefits of the Enterprise Risk Management implementation may be seen immediately in some departments; however, the same situation may not be realized in other departments of same company. I am determined as a mission to myself to be a pioneer by presenting books and other publications about Enterprise Risk Management in the airport/airline business.

The effective Enterprise Risk Management framework and related systems presents following benefits for the company:

- More effective decision making and strategic planning
- Increasing of profitability
- Minimizing of the surprises and well-prepared for the surprises
- determining of the strategies as more healthy
- Increasing of the investment's interest
- Quickly reaching of the effective risk data and related information
- Better determination of opportunities and threats
- Creating of value from uncertainties and instability
- Increasing of the competitive power
- Performing of the proactive management instead of the reactive management
- More effective allocation and using of the resources
- Providing to the distribution of the resource as more effectively
- Decreasing to the cost's of risks

- Decreasing of the damage and much better to the managing of the events
- Developing of the shareholder's confidence and reliance
- Providing of the compliance with laws and regulation as continually
- Tracing of the corporate performance as risk focusing
- Upgrading and improving of the corporate management.

The providing of these benefits is depends on the characteristics of the company and its effective implementation performance of the Enterprise Risk Management. The company can provide maximum benefit from the implementation of the Enterprise Risk Management if its best and the true determination of the corporate objectives, establishing the suitable Enterprise Risk Management systems and if it puts into practice the functions as parallel with the tailored Enterprise Risk Management framework. Enterprise Risk Management must be tailored according to the company. Every company has different characteristics, objectives, human resources, managerial attitude, etc. They should be considered to shape of the Enterprise Risk Management framework for each company. Enterprise Risk Management implementations and frameworks should be highly customized at each company such that the final framework is appropriate and reflects the complexity, size and sophistication of the company. Nevertheless, there are several key criteria to a successful Enterprise Risk Management framework. They are presented in the book.

The nature and scope of risks have changed. They are now complex, interconnected and global. Enterprise Risk Management is a necessity for companies so as to seek better decision-making and greater shareholder value. Enterprise Risk Management is the enabler for linking risk management processes with capital allocation and trading strategies that both protect and drive value creation. Good Enterprise Risk Management will deliver value creating compliance (SAS, 2006). In the business environment of nowadays, many forces occasionally make companies to view business risk across all their business operations. Globalization, technological drivers, competitive pressures, market expectations and the complexity of business models and relationships drive the essential demand for a more holistic approach to risk management. Additionally, regulatory scrutiny and mounting compliance costs push companies toward a comprehensive and strategic approach to risk management.

Enterprise Risk Management has been the topic of increased media attention in recent years. Many organizations carry out Enterprise Risk Management programs, consulting firms establish specialized Enterprise Risk Management units and universities develop Enterprise Risk Management -related courses and research centers. Unlike traditional risk management where individual risk categories are separately managed in risk 'silos', Enterprise Risk Management enables firms to manage a wide array of risks in an integrated, holistic fashion. More generally, Enterprise Risk Management is said to promote increased risk management awareness that translates into better operational and strategic decisions.

Risk cannot be eliminated for corporate sustainability and sustainable growth in a highly complex environment, but it can be managed. Companies readily appreciate that risk considerations have extended beyond finance and insurance to embrace strategic, operational, reputation, regulatory and information issues and that organizational effectiveness requires an improved fine agreement of the risks material to them.

Today, all businesses are risky. Companies face with a wide range of risks in the normal course of business. Nevertheless, not all risks are equally important. Enterprise Risk Management graciously assists the focus of the managers on the risks that has largest influence "both positive and negative" on their ability to achieve strategic goals and to add shareholder value. The objective of the book is to identify the best practices of risk management including strategies, approaches, methods, tools and techniques and how they can be used in the air transportation sector: Airline and airport business.

More importantly, the practice of risk management has shifted in fundamental way. In the past, companies managed risks by "silos," in which different types of risk--business, credit, market, operational--were managed by different organizational units. By time, risk management professionals recognized that risks, by their nature, are highly interdependent. As a matter of fact, major corporate disasters often caused not only by a single risk factor but also by a convergence of risk factors. This recognition has led to the development and implementation of integrated approaches to measuring and managing risks across the enterprise, also known as enterprise risk management. Enterprise Risk Management is a matter of future survival in an increasingly complex world. Implementation will vary from company to company depending on culture, leadership support, internal and external risk profile.

Enterprise Risk Management framework and related infrastructure are not one-size-fits-all. What works for one organization may not work for another. The elements of Enterprise Risk Management infrastructure vary according to the techniques and tools deployed to implement Enterprise Risk Management, the breadth of the objectives addressed, the culture of the organizations and the extent of coverage desired across the organization's operating units. Management should decide the elements of Enterprise Risk Management infrastructure needed according to these and other relevant factors. If it is properly carried out, Enterprise Risk Management can improve organizations to pursue strategic growth opportunities with greater speed, skill and confidence by aligning the risk taking of organizations with its core competencies and risk appetite. Markets notice strategically focused organizations and will differentiate these organizations by the quality and extent - real or perceived - of their risk management capabilities.

Enterprise Risk Management is **not** a **'one size fits all'** managerial approach or implementation. Enterprise risk management implementation structures are usually tailored to an individual company and reflect the nature, likelihood and magnitude of risk faced by the company. Concepts and implementations regarding enterprise risk management issues are very limited in both quantity and context, especially in the airport business. This book is prepared to offer the best Enterprise Risk Management concept and its samples with its conceptual concept. Furthermore, a new approach is presented to select of the best Enterprise Risk Management operator at the Airport Business in this book. This book is based on Doctorate Dissertation of Author **Dr. Ayse KUCUK YILMAZ: ENTERPRISE RISK MANAGEMENT IN THE AIRPORTS: THE MODEL SUGGESTION FOR THE ATATURK AIRPORTS TERMINAL OPERATIONS COMPANY,** Anadolu University, Eskisehir, Turkey, 2007.

Author's book offerings serve airport and airline companies align their strategies, processes, technology and knowledge with the definite aim of improving their capabilities to evaluate and manage - enterprise wide - the uncertainties, which they meet as they execute their business model. This book aims to answer to the following main questions:

i. What is the enterprise risk management (ERM) framework?
ii. What are the best ERM practices and related criteria?
iii. What are the best ERM practices in the airline business?
iv. How to select the best enterprise risk management operator in the airport business?

The book is organized into V chapters. **Chapter I,** Enterprise risk management fundamentals, benefits and enterprise risk management frameworks are presented. This is required to primarily observe the characteristics of Enterprise risk management implementation and its frameworks in the business management. Various enterprise risk management frameworks are presented in **Chapter II.** In **Chapter III** detailed information to the best practice of the enterprise risk management is given. In addition, general best ERM practice criteria are presented in this chapter. **Chapter IV** consists of the best samples of Enterprise Risk Management implementations in the airline and airport business. **Chapter V** is presented as a new approach to selection of the best operator about enterprise risk management practice at airport business. In this chapter, criteria to the best enterprise risk management practice are determined by the author. Criteria are identified in four main categories: benefits, costs, opportunities and risks of enterprise risk management implementation. Fundamentally, the target of the book is just to give a direction to the best enterprise risk management implementation in the air transportation sector: airline and airport business.

There is not a single best practice or a unique model to Enterprise Risk Management. Enterprise Risk Management frameworks are created according to the organizational objectives, strategy, culture and characteristics. This book provides an overview of the Enterprise Risk Management framework and its best practices in the air transportation.

This book is second step in my enterprise risk management journey. This is a risky way and is full of opportunities for me.

Dr. Ayse KUCUK YILMAZ
Turkey, 2008.

DEDICATION

Dr. Ayse KUCUK YILMAZ

This second book is dedicated to my husband, Mehmet Yilmaz and my mother, Ferziye; my father, Mehmet; My sister, Alev and my brother, Ali Ihsan Kucuk. Without their love, encouragement and support, this journey to advance my academic carrier would have been extremely more difficult and meanless.

I believe that my books are wonderful starting points for my professional carrier journey. Also, publishing these books give me an amazing opportunity to show my understanding of Enterprise Risk Management across the world. So, I want to thank for VDM publishing house for support.

CHAPTER 1

"ONE SIZE DOES NOT FIT ALL"

SHAPING OF ERM FRAMEWORKS

CHAPTER 1

ONE SIZE DOES NOT FIT ALL!

1. **INTRODUCTION**

The need for Enterprise Risk Management (ERM) has become more vital than ever in the today's business environment. ERM is a systematic and proactive approach for evaluating and monitoring risk and opportunity. In the risky world, companies can no longer rely on a silo approach for risk management but need an integrated and holistic perspective of all the risks facing the organization (University of Virginia, Oct 2006).

Companies realize the business value of managing risk across the enterprises effectively in different ways. Enterprise risk departments establish and led at remarkable speed by risk staff with impressive analytical capabilities and risk certifications (Minsky, 2006).

Risk is a necessary part of doing business, and the management of risk has become a vital function of every enterprise as a matter of corporate survival.

ERM is the corporate-wide application of risk management to improve the functioning of the business an organization. Understanding the risk and making informed decisions in response to uncertainty are fundamental while seeking to build a robust and deliverable business strategy. ERM is something more than crisis management or regulatory compliance. It is a tangible and structured approach for addressing organizational and financial risk. ERM, ultimately, works towards enhancing shareholder value and competitive advantage (KPMG, 2007).

ERM is the latest name for an overall risk management approach to business risks. Precursors to this term include corporate risk management, business risk management, holistic risk management, strategic risk management and integrated risk management. Although each of these terms has a slightly different focus, partially fostered by the risk elements that are of primary concern to organizations when each term is first emerged, the general concepts are quite similar (D'Arcy, 2001).

In business, ERM refers to the methods and processes used by organizations to manage risks (or seize opportunities) related to the achievement of their objectives. ERM provides a rigorous framework for risk management, which typically involves identifying particular events or circumstances relevant to the organization's objectives (risks and opportunities), assessing them in terms of likelihood and magnitude of impact, determining a response strategy, and monitoring progress. By identifying and proactively addressing risks and opportunities, business enterprises protect and create value for their stakeholders, including owners, employees, customers, regulators and society overall.

ERM is evolves to address the essential demands of various stakeholders, who want to see the broad spectrum of risks taken by complex organizations to ensure that they are appropriately managed. Regulators and debt rating agencies have increased their scrutiny on the risk management processes of companies.

ERM enables an organization to deal effectively with uncertainty and associated risk. ERM is a systematic approach for identifying and managing the business risks of an organization. ERM offers a proven method to align risk appetite with strategic goals, deploys resources more effectively, reduces operational surprises and losses, and improves risk response (PriceWaterhouseCoopers, 2007).

Unlike traditional risk management, ERM avoids this silo mentality by using a root cause approach to rightfully take a comprehensive view of risk. Leading corporations quickly adopt ERM therefore. However, some corporations are slow to adopt ERM best practices and extend their programs to line management. According to a recent survey, although 70 percent of corporations say they intend to adopt ERM in the next few years, and many organizations have not met their ERM goals (Minsky, 2006).

According to the Casualty Actuarial Society (CAS), ERM is defined as: "The process by which organizations in all industries assess, control, exploit, finance and monitor risks from all sources for increasing the organization's short and long term value to its stakeholders." The CAS then proceeds to enumerate the types of risk subject to enterprise risk management as hazard, financial, operational and strategic. Hazard risks are those risks that have traditionally been addressed by insurers, including fire, theft, windstorm, liability, business interruption, pollution, health and pensions. Financial risks cover potential losses in consequences of changes in financial markets, including interest rates, foreign exchange rates, commodity prices, liquidity risks and credit risk. Operational risks cover a wide variety of situations, including customer satisfaction, product development, product failure, trademark protection, corporate leadership, information technology, management fraud and information risk. Strategic risks include such factors as completion, customer preferences, technological innovation and regulatory or political impediments. Although there can be disagreement over which category would apply to a specific instance, the primary point is that ERM considers all types of risk an organization face . A common thread of ERM is that the overall risks of the professional systems are managed in aggregate, rather than independently. Risk is also viewed as a potential profit opportunity, rather than as something simply to be minimized or eliminated. The level of decision making under ERM is also shifted, from the insurance risk manager, who would generally seek to control risk, to the chief executive officer, or board of directors, who would be willing to embrace profitable risk opportunities (Kawamoto, 2001).

ERM aligns strategy, people, processes, technology and knowledge with the objective of continuously improving the organisation's risk management capabilities over time (Protiviti, 2006). The COSO Enterprise Risk Management - Integrated Framework, issued in September 2004, defines ERM as follows: A process, affected by an entity's board of directors, management and other personnel; applied in strategy setting and across the enterprise, designed to identify potential events that may affect the entity, and manage risk to be within its risk appetite, to provide reasonable assurance regarding the achievement of entity objectives.

Note that the context of the above definition is strategy setting. The application is enterprise wide. The standard is the risk appetite of the enterprises.

ERM improves capabilities of the company for managing its priority risks. When an ERM approach is effectively integrated to strategy-setting, the attention of the management is directed to the uncertainties affecting entire asset portfolio of the enterprise, including its customer assets, its employee/supplier assets and such organizational assets as its differentiating strategies, distinctive products and brands and innovative processes and systems. This expanded focus is important in this era of market capitalization to significantly exceed balance sheet values and is also important for the desire of many companies to reduce the risk of reputation loss to an acceptable level.

All organizations face with uncertainty; the challenge for management is to determine how much uncertainty should be accepted. Uncertainty presents both risk and opportunity, with the potential to erode or enhance the value of the organization. Enterprise risk management assists a professional system to arrive where it wants to avoid pitfalls and surprises along the way.

ERM is clearly defined by COSO (Committee of Sponsoring Organizations of the Treadway Commission) as a process designed to (1) identify potential events that may affect the organization, (2) manage risk to be within the organization's risk appetite, and (3) provide reasonable assurance regarding the achievement of the organization's objectives.

Within the context of the organization's established mission, management establishes strategic objectives, selects strategy, and sets aligned objectives cascading through the enterprise. The ERM framework is geared to achieving the organization's objectives, set forth in four categories (COSO, 2004):

- **Strategic** - high-level goals, aligned with and supporting its mission.
- **Operations** - effective and efficient use of its resources
- **Reporting** - reliability of reporting
- **Compliance** - compliance with applicable laws and regulations.

ERM consists of eight interrelated components. These are derived from the way management runs an enterprise and are integrated with the management process. These components are (COSO, 2004):

• **Internal Environment** - The internal environment encompasses the tone of an organization, and sets the base for how risk is viewed and addressed by an organization's people, including the risk management philosophy and risk appetite, integrity and ethical values, and the environment in which they operate.

• **Objective Setting** - Objectives must exist before management can identify potential events affecting their achievement. Enterprise risk management ensures that management has in place a process to set objectives and that the chosen objectives support and align with the organization's mission and are consistent with its risk appetite.

• **Event Identification** - Internal and external events affecting achievement of an organization's objectives must be identified, distinguishing between risks and opportunities. Opportunities are channeled back to management's strategy or objective-setting processes.

• **Risk Assessment** - Risks are analyzed, considering likelihood and impact, as a basis for determining how they should be managed. Risks are assessed on both an inherent basis and a residual basis.

• **Risk Response** - Management selects risk responses - avoiding, accepting, reducing, or sharing risk - developing a set of actions to align risks with the entity's risk tolerances and risk appetite.

• **Control Activities** - Policies and procedures are established and carried out to assist ensure the risk responses are effectively carried out.

• **Information and Communication** - Relevant information is identified, captured, and knowingly passed in a form and duration that enables people to carry out their responsibilities. Effective communication also occurs in a broader sense, flowing down, across, and up the entity.

- **Monitoring** - The entirety of enterprise risk management (ERM) is monitored and modifications made as necessary. Monitoring is accomplished through ongoing management activities, separate evaluations, or both.

ERM is not strictly a serial process, where one component affects only the next process. It is a multidirectional, iterative process in which almost any component can and does influence another. There is a direct relationship among objectives, which is what an organization strives to achieve, and ERM components, which represent what is needed to achieve them. The relationship is depicted in a three-dimensional matrix, as a cube. The four objectives categories - strategic, operations, reporting, and compliance - are represented by the vertical columns, the eight components by horizontal rows, and the organization's units by the third dimension. This depiction portrays the required ability to focus on the entirety of an organization's enterprise risk management, or by objectives category, component, organizational unit, or any subset thereof.

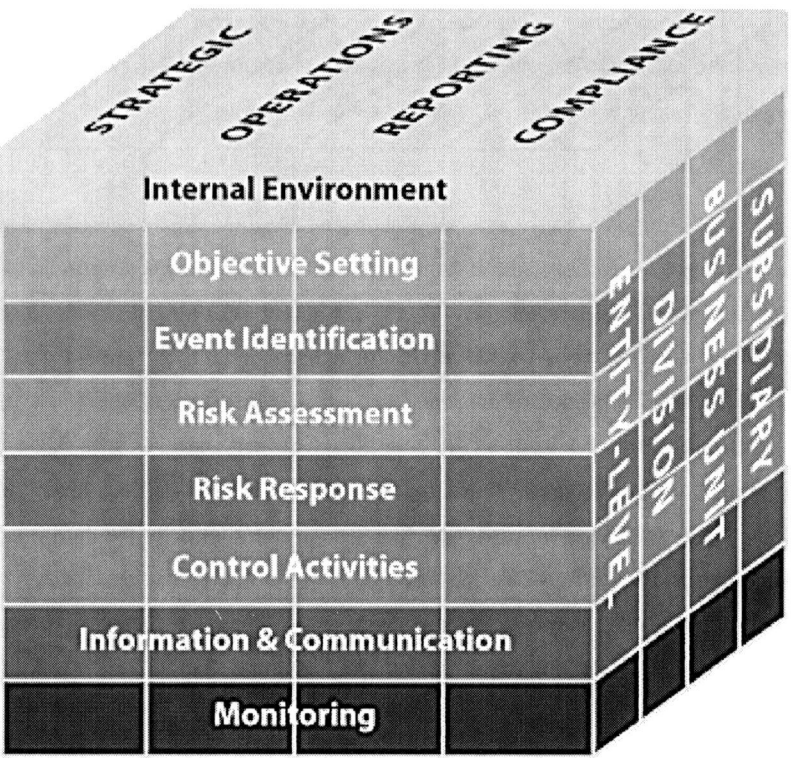

Figure-1. COSO Enterprise Risk Management Cube (www.coso.org).

Determining whether the ERM is "effective" is a judgment resulting from an assessment of whether the eight components are present and functioning effectively. Thus, the components are also criteria for the effective ERM. For the components to be present and functioning properly there can be no material weaknesses, and risk needs to have been brought within the risk appetite of the organization. When the ERM is determined to be effective in each of the four categories of objectives, respectively, senior management has reasonable assurance that they understand the extent to which the entity's strategic and operations objectives are being achieved and that the organization's reporting is reliable and applicable laws and regulations are being complied with.

2. BENEFITS OF ENTERPRISE RISK MANAGEMENT

No entity occasionally operates in a risk-free environment, and ERM does not create such an environment. Rather, ERM enables management to occasionally operate more effectively in environments filled with risks. ERM provides enhanced capability to (COSO, ERM Framework, 2004):

Align risk appetite and strategy - Risk appetite is the degree of risk, on a broad-based level, that a company or other entities is willing to accept in pursuit of its goals. Management considers the entity's risk appetite first in evaluating strategic alternatives, then in setting objectives aligned with the selected strategy and in developing mechanisms to manage the related risks.

Link growth, risk and return - Entities accept risk as part of value creation and preservation, and they expect return commensurate with the risk. ERM generously offers an enhanced ability to identify and assess risks, and establish acceptable levels of risk relative to be growth and return objectives.

Enhance risk response decisions - ERM provides the rigor to identify and select among alternative risk responses - risk avoidance, reduction, sharing and acceptance. ERM provides methodologies and techniques for making these decisions.

Minimize operational surprises and losses - Entities have enhanced capability to identify potential events, assess risk and establish responses, thereby reducing the occurrence of surprises and related costs or losses.

Identify and manage cross-enterprise risks - Every entity faces a myriad risk affecting different parts of the professional system. Management needs to not only manage individual risks, but also understand interrelated impacts.

Provide integrated responses to multiple risks - Business processes carry many inherent risks, and enterprise risk management enables integrated solutions for managing the risks.

Seize opportunities - Management considers potential events, rather than just risks, and by considering a full range of events, management gains an understanding of how certain events represent opportunities.

Rationalize capital - More robust information on an entity's total risk actively provides management to more effectively assess overall capital needs and improve capital allocation.

ERM is not an end in itself, but important means. It cannot and does not operate in isolation in an entity, but an enable of the management process. ERM is interrelated with corporate governance by providing information to the board of directors on the most significant risks and how they are being managed. And, it interrelates with performance management by providing risk-adjusted measures, and with internal control, which is an integral part of ERM. ERM gradually assists entities achieve its performance and profitability targets, and prevent loss of resources. It improves to ensure effective reporting. And, it graciously assists to ensure that the entity complies with laws and regulations, avoiding damage to its reputation and other consequences. In sum, it helps entities get to where it wants to go to avoid pitfalls and surprises along the way (COSO, 2004).

3. IMPORTANCE OF ENTERPRISE RISK MANAGEMENT

As the dynamics of the market, business environment and changes in regulatory requirements for corporations increase in their complexity, it becomes harder to plot the right course for continued success. The abilities to identify and to adapt to changes are key success factors for the leaders of tomorrow. Considering this, companies are driven more than ever by the desire to protect their reputation and manage their risks effectively. ERM generously offers a rigorous model for management to deal effectively with uncertainty and associated risk and opportunity, thereby enhancing its capacity of build value (PricewaterhouseCoopers-PwC, 2006).

ERM does not operate in isolation environment in the corporation, but it is an enable in the management process. ERM is part of corporate governance by providing information to the board of directors and to the audit committee on the most significant risks and how they are being managed. It interrelates with performance management by providing risk-adjusted measures, and with internal control, which is an integral part of enterprise risk management (PwC, 2006).

Best practices in corporate governance begin with a commitment by the board of directors and senior managers to elevate the discipline to a high strategic priority. To improve corporate governance and make it a primary source of value, leading companies integrate their governance, risk management and compliance activities, so they are more efficient, consistent and legally sound. To create this integrated governance and risk management model, the companies identify and prioritize risks that need to be managed and controlled, launch change management initiatives to support the necessary structural and job changes, and enable and measure this transformation through the information technology (IT) infrastructure (PwC, 2006).

Traditional risk management approaches tend to be fragmented, compartmentalizing risks into silos. These approaches often limit the focus to managing uncertainties around physical and financial assets. Because they focus largely on loss prevention, rather than enhancing enterprise value, traditional approaches do not provide the extended model most organizations need to redefine the risk management value proposition in a rapidly changing world. ERM, on the other hand, provides an organization with the process it needs to become more anticipatory and effective at evaluating and managing the uncertainties it faces as it creates sustainable value for stakeholders. ERM improves an organization manage its risks to protect and enhance enterprise value in three ways (Protiviti, 2007):

- First, it focuses on establishing sustainable competitive advantage. ERM improves management overcome silo behaviour by aligning views of risk and enabling the enterprise to respond successfully to a changing environment. ERM elevates risk management to a strategic level by broadening the application and focus of the risk management process to all sources of enterprise value, not just physical and financial ones.

- Second, it optimizes the multiple cost of managing risk. Through ERM, management aggregates risk acceptance and transfer decisions, eliminates redundant activities and determines the current level of risk the organization is prepared to accept as it executes its business model.

- Third, it assists management improve business performance. ERM improves management with reducing unacceptable performance variability and loss exposure by (a) expecting the impact of major events and (b) initially getting responses to prevent those events from occurring and manage their impact on the system if they do occur. ERM transitions risk management from "avoiding and hedging bets" to a differentiating skill for protecting and enhancing enterprise value as management seeks to make the best bets in the pursuit of new opportunities for growth and return.

ERM invigorates opportunity-seeking behaviour by aiding managers develop the confidence that they truly understand the risks they are taking on and have the capabilities at hand within the organization to manage those risks. Our research over the years, including our recently issued Protiviti U.S. Risk Barometer (available at www.protiviti.co. uk), consistently shows that six of ten senior executives "lack high confidence" that their company's risk management practices identify and manage all potentially significant business risks. The focus of ERM is on integrating risk management with strategy-setting. The emphasis is on identifying future potential events that can have both positive and negative affects and evaluating effective strategies for managing the organization's exposure to those future events. ERM transforms risk management to a proactive, continuous, value-based, broadly focused and process-driven activity. These contributions redefine the value proposition of risk management to a business.

Five steps to carrying out ERM for organizations choosing to implement ERM, we recommend five practical steps. While the following steps provide a simplified view of the task of carrying out ERM, the implementation process does not occur overnight. ERM is a journey and these steps provide a practical starting point.

STEP 1: Conduct an enterprise risk assessment (ERA) Using the business strategy as a context, a ERA identifies and prioritizes the organization's risk and provides quality inputs for purposes of formulating effective risk responses, including information about the current state of capabilities around managing the priority risks. If an organization has not prioritized its risks, ERM becomes a tough sell because the value proposition can only be generic. Identifying gaps relating to the entity's priority risks provide the basis for improving the specificity of the ERM value proposition. Consequently, avoid endless dialogues about ERM: Get started by conducting a ERA to understand the risks inherent in your business model.

STEP 2: Articulate the ERM vision and value proposition using gaps around the priority risks. This step provides the economic justification for going forward. The ERM vision is a shared view of the role of risk management in the organization and the capabilities needed to manage its key risks. A working group of senior executives should be empowered to (a) articulate the role of risk management in the organization and (b) define relevant goals and objectives for the enterprise as a whole and its business units. To accomplish this task, management needs a reliable fact base grounded in specific capabilities that must be developed to improve risk management performance. This is where a gap analysis becomes handy. To illustrate:

(A) Begin with prioritizing the critical risks and determine the current state of capabilities around managing those risks. This is a ERA, as discussed in Step 1. Once the current state of overall capabilities is determined for each of the key risks, the desired state is assessed with the object of identifying gaps and advancing the maturity of risk management capabilities to close those gaps. "Risk management capabilities" include the policies, processes, competencies, reports, methodologies and technology basically took to execute the organization's risk response.

(B) ERM infrastructure consists of the policies, processes, organizational structure and reporting in place to instil the appropriate oversight, control and discipline around continuously improving risk management capabilities. Examples of elements of ERM infrastructure include, among other things, an overall risk management policy, an enterprise wide risk assessment process, presence of risk management on the Board and CEO agenda, a chartered risk committee, clarity of risk management roles and responsibilities, dashboard and other risk reporting, and proprietary tools that portray a portfolio view of risk. Here is the message: The greater the gap between the current state and the desired state of the organization's risk management capabilities (Point (A) above), the greater the need for ERM infrastructure (Point (B) above) to facilitate the advancement of those risk management capabilities over time.

STEP 3: Advance the risk management capabilities of the organization for one or two priority risks. This step focuses the organisation on improving its risk management capabilities in an area where management knows improvements are needed. Like any other initiative, ERM must begin somewhere. There are many possible starting points. Examples include:

• One or two priority financial or operational risks based on the enterprise wide risk assessment results (sees Step 1), e.g., operational risk in a financial institution

• Regulatory compliance risks and/or governance reform issues

• Integration of ERM with the management processes that matter, e.g., strategic management, annual business planning, new product launch or channel expansion, quality initiatives, capital expenditure planning and performance measurement and assessment

Regardless of where an organization begins its journey, the focus of ERM is the same - to advance the maturity of risk management capabilities for the priority business risks.

STEP 4: Evaluate the existing ERM infrastructure capability and develop a strategy to advance it It takes oversight, control and discipline to advance the capabilities around managing the critical risks. The policies, processes, organization and reporting that instil that oversight, control and discipline are called "ERM infrastructure." The purpose of ERM infrastructure is to eliminate significant gaps between the current state and the desired state of the organization's capabilities around managing its key risks. We provided some examples of ERM infrastructure above when discussing Step 2. Other examples include a common risk language, knowledge sharing of best practices, common training, a chief risk officer (or equivalent executive), definition of risk appetite and risk tolerances, integration of risk responses with business plans, and supporting technology.

ERM infrastructure facilitates three indispensable things with respect to ERM implementation. First, it establishes fact-based understanding about the enterprise's risks and risk management capabilities. Second, it ensures there is ownership over the critical risks. Finally, it drives closure of unacceptable gaps. ERM infrastructure is not a one-size-fits-all. What works for one organization might not work for another. The elements of ERM infrastructure vary according to the techniques and tools deployed to implement ERM, the breadth of the objectives addressed, the organization's culture and the extent of coverage desired across the organization's operating units. Management should decide the elements of ERM infrastructure needed according to these and other relevant factors.

STEP 5: Advance the risk management capabilities for other key risks. After the first four steps are completed, it will often be necessary to update the ERA for change. Once there is a refined definition of the priority risks, based on the updated ERA, management must determine the current state of the capabilities for managing each risk and then assess the desired state. The objective is the same as with the one or two priority risks addressed in Step 3, i.e., to advance the maturity of the enterprise's capabilities around managing its key risks. In taking this step, management broadens the enterprise's focus to other priority risks.

Improving risk management capability is the aim for each priority risk; management evaluates the relative maturity of the enterprise's capabilities. From there, management needs to make a conscious decision: How much added capability do we need to continuously achieve our performance goals and objectives? Improvements in risk management capabilities must be designed and advanced, consistent with the organization's finite resources and management's assessment of the expected costs and benefits. The ultimate goal is to identify the organization's most pressing strategic exposures and uncertainties and to focus the advance of capabilities for managing them. The ERM infrastructure management has preferably preferred to put in place drives progress towards this goal.

Companies in the early stages of developing their ERM infrastructure often set the needy basis with a common language, a risk management oversight structure and an enterprise risk assessment process. Some companies have applied ERM within specific business units. Furthermore, a few companies have evolved towards more advanced stages, such as the management of market and credit risks in financial institutions and the management of compliance risks in regulated industries. Wherever a company stands with respect to developing its risk management, directors and management would benefit from a dialogue around how capable the entity's risk management needs to be with respect to each its priority risks using the business strategy as a context. Various, consulting firms offer suggestions for how to implement the ERM programme. Common topics and challenges include as follows:

i. Establishing a common risk language or terminology
ii. Establishing ERM-based culture
iii. Tailoring and shaping of ERM framework
iv. Establishing best ERM function and committee
v. Integrating of ERM to corporate managerial approach, strategy and functions.

4. LIMITATIONS OF ENTERPRISE RISK MANAGEMENT

Effective ERM serves to achieve for management objectives. Nevertheless, ERM, no matter how well designed and operated, does not ensure an entity's success. The achievement of objectives is affected by limitations inherent in all management processes. Shifts in government policy or programs, competitors' actions or economic conditions can be beyond management's control. Human decision making can be faulty, and breakdowns can occur as a result of such human failures as simple error or mistake. ERM cannot change an inherently poor manager into a good one. Additionally, controls can be circumvented by the collusion of two or more people, and management can override the ERM process, including risk responses and controls. The design of ERM must reflect the reality of resource constraints, and the risk management benefits must be correctly taking relative to their costs. Thus, while ERM can improve management achieve its objectives, it is not a panacea (COSO, 2004).

CHAPTER II

ERM FRAMEWORKS

CHAPTER II

ENTERPRISE RISK MANAGEMENT FRAMEWORK

1. INTRODUCTION

Enterprise Risk Management (ERM) is a globally accepted and growing field, and as a result, several risk frameworks and statements have been published by professional organizations around the world. Some of the publications encourage enterprises to use these frameworks. Other risk frameworks have a "comply or explain why not" approach. Still other frameworks are legally mandated or implied in their respective countries. Some of the documents are written by accounting and auditing organizations such as COSO, while others are written by individuals with a wider range of backgrounds such as insurance, government, safety and engineering. The different backgrounds lead to very different approaches in these risk frameworks. Enterprise risk management frameworks are valuable tools. They usually provide a diagram or approach that includes the steps necessary for ERM implementation besides providing guidance and examples (IMA, 2006).

Companies continue to face with increasing pressures to implement ERM processes. Both industry and government regulatory bodies, as well as investors, are increasingly examining these policies and processes. Boards of directors in an increasing of number of industries are now required to review and report the effectiveness of ERM frameworks in their companies.

ERM also takes part as a framework for corporate business practices. When researched to rank the highest priority objectives of the companies for ERM implementations, companies carefully put the greatest emphasis on "ensuring risks are considered in decision making" and "avoiding surprises and predictable failures", reflecting the interest of companies in their ability to discover and use critical risk information.

ERM implementation and related frameworks should emphasize strategy-setting. ERM practice depends on the priority risks of each company which are defined in the context of its business strategy and the gaps are also defined around managing those risks. Management must decide the nature of the ERM framework based on the size, objectives, strategy, structure, culture, management style, risk profile, industry, competitive environment and financial wherewithal of the organizations. These and other factors affect how the ERM framework is applied (Protiviti, 2006).

ERM is certainly not only a project management discipline, but also it is much more than a project. ERM is a journey, meaning it is a growth process in which the organization integrates risk management to strategy-setting to improve the effectiveness of its enterprise risk management capabilities over time.

The length of time basically needed to implement ERM varies, depending on the current state of the risk management of the organization, its desired future state and the extent to which it wishes to dedicate resources to improve risk management capabilities. In addition, because ERM requires an open environment relation to effective communication about risks and risk management up, down and across the enterprise, cultural subjects may exist for many organizations to overcome. For example, ERM requires an elimination of barriers -functional or departmental- so that a truly holistic, integrated, proactive, forward-looking and process-oriented approach is adopted to manage all key business risks and opportunities - not just financial ones. If there are significant change management subjects to address, the period to implement ERM will be extended (Protiviti, 2006). While, the completion of the applications taken into consideration takes twelve months time in any organization, most organizations will basically need from three to five years to reach their objectives in fully carrying out their ERM framework and related systems.

The policies, processes, organization and reporting that instils that discipline is called "ERM infrastructure". The purpose of ERM infrastructure is to eliminate significant gaps among the current state and the desired state of the organization capabilities within the content of its fundamental risks. Some examples of ERM infrastructure exist. Examples include a common risk language and other frameworks, knowledge sharing to identify best practices, common training, a chief risk officer (or equivalent executive), definition of risk appetite and risk tolerances, integration of risk responses with business plans and supporting technology.

ERM infrastructure is not one-size-fits-all. What works for one may not work for others. The elements of ERM infrastructure vary according to the techniques and tools to implement the ERM framework, the breadth of the objectives addressed, the culture of the organization and risk appetite, the nature of its risks and the extent of coverage desired across the operating units of the organization. Management decides the elements of ERM infrastructure needed according to these and other factors. When making this decision, management considers that the element of ERM infrastructure is already in its place (Protiviti, 2006).

ERM is not a kind of project. ERM is a journey because it presents a commitment to a continuous improvement. Because the risks of an organization constantly change, its risk management capabilities must be constantly improved (Protiviti, FAQ, 2006). ERM provides the focus, discipline and control for the context of the strategy setting process takes place on time.

Each organization must design its own enterprise risk management framework, process, roles and responsibilities, documentation, and so forth. However, there are standard enterprise risk management functional elements for framework, procedures, etc. which should be used in the design. This ensures that the risk management procedures will be recognizable to others and will improve both effectiveness and efficiency. Chapter two presents selected ERM frameworks and their elements. This chapter will also introduce several frameworks that represent the current state-of-the-art and have application as a way of enhancing the basic conceptualization of an "ERM framework".

A study of the various ERM definitions reveals that all share three critical characteristics (Abrams et. all, 2007):

1. Integrated-ERM must span all lines of business.
2. Comprehensive-ERM must include all types of risks.
3. Strategic-ERM must be aligned with overall business tactics.

As companies perform risk management, they typically come to the conclusion that they cannot manage risk in an ad hoc manner by vertical business unit, by specific regulation, or by domain; it becomes apparent that risk management must be conducted in a structured manner and integrated throughout the whole enterprise. This includes several elements, such as the definition of risk, the formation of a risk oversight role, defined tolerances, policies and procedures for dealing with risk, the inclusion of risk as a factor in business decision making, and the reporting of risk in a consistent manner.

Furthermore, ERM must be comprehensive and include all risks to understand and manage the interplay among various types of risks and certain events which have more than one types of risk should be taken into consideration. Furthermore, risk must be managed from a business strategy point of view. Not all risk is bad, and the business strategy must set a risk appetite policy to govern the ERM approach. For example, the airtransportation industry lives by taking risk and managing it.

The framework describes the critical principles and components of an effective enterprise risk management process, setting forth how all important risks should be identified, assessed, responded and controlled. It also provides a common language, so that when executives, directors and others talk about risk management, they are truly communicating. The framework sets for how a company applies enterprise risk management in its strategic planning and also describes techniques some companies use in identifying and managing risk. The framework emphasizes how an effective enterprise risk management process identifies not only the downside, but also the upside, or the opportunities that can be seized to enhance profitability and return. The framework also describes roles of key players in the ERM process.

2. SAMPLES OF ENTERPRISE RISK MANAGEMENT FRAMEWORK

ERM frameworks describe an approach for identifying, analyzing, responding to, and monitoring risks or opportunities, within the internal and external environment the enterprise faces with. Management selects a risk response strategy for specific risks identified and analyzed, which may include (Wikipedia, 2007):

i. Avoidance : existing the actions definitely contributing rise to risk

ii. Reduction: taking action to reduce the likelihood or impact related to the risk.

iii. Share or insure: transferring or sharing a portion of the risk to reduce it.

iv. Accept: no action taken, as a result of the cost/benefit decision.

In this section, the following ERM frameworks are briefly discussed:

- The Combined Code and Turnbull Guidance
- King II Report
- A Risk Management Standard by the Federation of European Risk Management
- Association (FERMA)
- Australian/New Zealand Standard 4360—Risk Management
- COSO's Enterprise Risk Management—Integrated Framework
- The Institute of Management Accountants' (IMA) "A Global Perspective on Assessing Internal Control over Financial Reporting" (ICoFR)
- Basel II

- Standard & Poor's and ERM
- Risk and Insurance Management Society (RIMS) Risk Maturity Model
- AIRMIC
- Transport Canada
- Japaneese Industrial Risk Management Standard
- British Standard
- FAA Safety Risk Management

Selected ERM frameworks are examined in the following part of this chapter.

2.1. The Combined Code and Turnbull Guidance

In the United Kingdom, the Financial Reporting Council published the *Combined Code on Corporate Governance* (the Code) in 2003. Although the Code is not specifically labeled as an ERM framework, it does have many similar aspects, and "risk" is mentioned more than 100 times. The Code states that the role of the board is to provide a framework of effective control so that risk is assessed and managed. The board is also required to review the effectiveness of controls, including all controls over financial, operational, and compliance areas as well as risk management systems. In 2005, the Financial Reporting Council also published Internal Control—Revised Guidance for Directors on the Combined Code, which is a revision of the Turnbull report first published in 1999. This guidance assumes that a company's board uses a risk-based approach to internal control. The guidance suggests that to assess a company's risk and control processes, the following elements must be reviewed:

- Risk assessment;
- Control environment and control activities;
- Information and communication; and
- Monitoring.

The guidance offers sample questions that could be used to assess the effectiveness of risk and control processes. Questions related to risk assessment focus on the presence of clear objectives, effective direction on risk assessment, measurable performance targets, identification and assessment of all risks on an ongoing basis, and a clear understanding of acceptable risks.

2.2. King II Report

The King Report on Corporate Governance for South Africa (King II Report) was published in 2002 to promote corporate governance. This report has five sections:

- Board and directors;
- Risk management;
- Internal audit;
- Integrated sustainability reporting; and
- Accounting and auditing.

The King II Report also includes an appendix on "risk management and internal controls." According to this report, the board is responsible for the risk management process and its effectiveness. The board should:

- Set risk strategy policies;
- Assess the risk process;
- Assess the risk exposures, such as physical and operational risks, human resource risks, technology risks, business continuity and disaster recovery, credit and market risks, and compliance risks;
- Review the risk management process and significant risks facing the company; and
- Be responsible for risk management disclosures.

2.3. A Risk Management Standard by the Federation of European Risk Management Association (FERMA)

A consortium of U.K. Organizations, including the Institute of Risk Management, the Association of Insurance and Risk Managers, and the National Forum for Risk Management in the Public Sector, published *A Risk Management Standard* (RMS) in 2004. The RMS represents best practices that companies can compare themselves against to determine how well they are doing in the prescribed areas. It is not a lengthy document, but it does provide a risk management process, which includes:

- Linkage to the organization's strategic objectives;
- Risk assessment, which the RMS breaks down into risk analysis, risk identification, risk description, risk estimation, and risk evaluation;
- Risk reporting;
- Decision;
- Risk treatment;
- Residual risk reporting; and
- Monitoring.

2.4. Australian/New Zealand Standard 4360—Risk Management

Australia and New Zealand formed a joint technical committee composed of representatives from numerous organizations to publish two documents on risk management in 2004. The committee is diverse and includes groups that focus on computers, customs, insurance, defense, emergency management, safety, securities, and accounting among many others. The first document is a standard entitled *Risk Management* (the Standard), which was initially published in 1999, and the second companion document entitled *Risk Management Guidelines* (the Guidance) provides insights on implementing the Standard. 26. The Standard can be applied to any type of organization and to any project or product. It attempts to factor in both the upside and downside of risk. Although the Standard specifies the elements of risk management, it is not intended to enforce uniformity. The Standard's aim is to provide direction in several areas, some of which are: a basis for decision-making, better risk identification, gaining value, resource allocation, improved compliance, and corporate governance. The Standard's risk management process is presented in Figure-2.

Figure-2 illustrates the Australian-New Zealand standard framework of functional processes (AS/NZS, 2004). It has a core set of functions that mirror those in Figure-2, with slightly different terminology, including the idea of extensive feedback loops and continuous monitoring. Like the Canadian framework, it explicitly identifies the "communicate and consult" function. The Australian-New Zealand framework introduced the concept of "Context" which is a further development of the Canadian "Initiation" step. Context provides the essential linkage among decision-makers and the technical or scientific analysis of risks. It is described as a process to "Establish the strategic, organizational and risk management context in which the rest of the process will take place. Criteria against which risk will be evaluated should be established and the structure of the analysis defined."

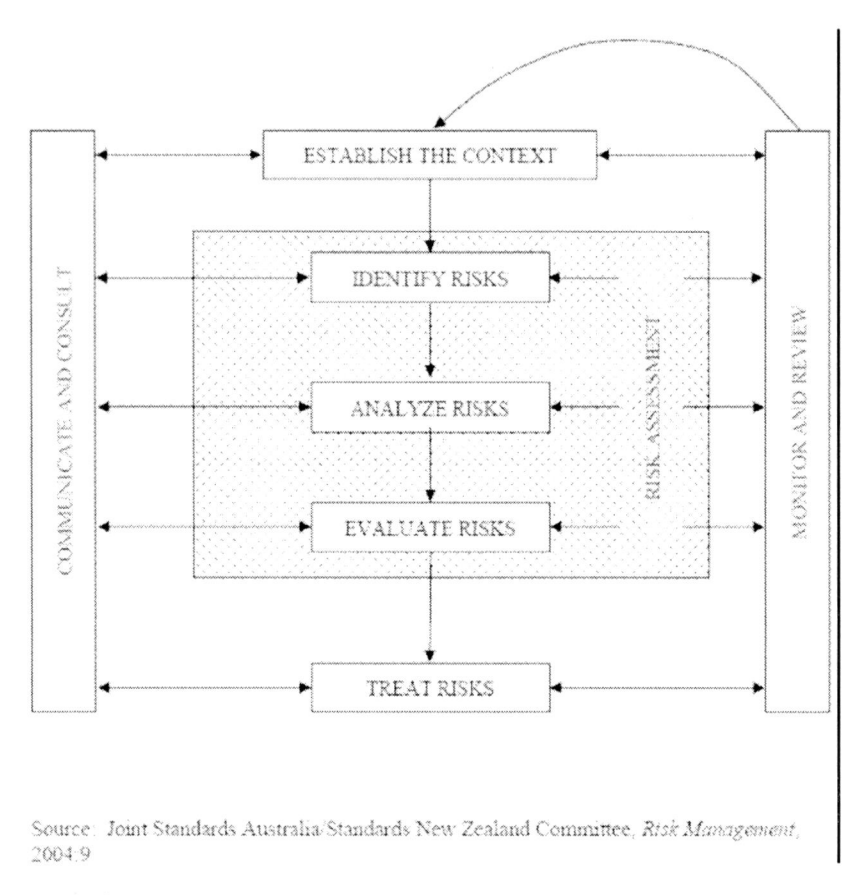

Figure-2. The Australian-New Zealand standard framework of functional processes (AS/NZS, 2004)

2.5. COSO's Enterprise Risk Management-Integrated Framework

COSO published in 1992 *Internal Control- Integrated Framework*, and in 2004, followed with publication of the ERM framework (see Exhibits two and 3). As noted previously in paragraph nine, the COSO definition of ERM is very broad. The ERM framework is clearly distinct from COSO's internal control framework. Interestingly, despite being more current, the SEC requires these companies comply with COSO's internal control framework rather than the ERM framework in meeting the SOX 404 requirements. The ERM framework notes that internal control is a part of ERM. The

COSO ERM framework has an eight interrelated component (see Figure-3-Figure-4). According to COSO's ERM framework, internal environment refers to the tone of the organisation, its risk appetite and elements such as oversight by the board. The framework states these companies comply must set objectives at the strategic level and must identify the risks and opportunities that impact the entity. Risks must then be assessed, and a response to the risk made-avoidance, reduction, sharing, or possibly acceptance. Clearly, COSO's ERM framework is one of the most comprehensive frameworks. COSO also published "application techniques" to supplement the framework. This document provides examples to gradually assist companies in carrying out ERM. For example, related to the internal environment component, the application techniques document shows sample risk management philosophy statements and illustrative codes of conduct. Other examples are given for each of the framework's components.

KEY ELEMENTS OF EACH COSO COMPONENT

Left Column	Internal Environment	Right Column
• Objectives and strategies organized by function and by unit • Key performance indicators organized by function and by unit • Risk tolerances and limits	**Internal Environment** Risk Management Philosophy • Risk Appetite • Board of Directors Integrity and Ethical Values • Commitment to Competence Organizational Structure • Assignment of Authority and Responsibility • Human Resource Standards	• Existing management oversight structure • Existing governance processes • Overall risk management vision • Enterprise risk management policy • Board reports • Periodic internal environment reviews
• Risk profile (significance, likelihood, financial impact) • Priority risks and unacceptable gaps	**Objective-Setting** Strategic Objectives • Related Objectives • Selected Objectives Risk Appetite • Risk Tolerances	
• Results of periodic self-assessments by managers and process and risk owners • Documented interrelationships • Key risk sources or drivers	**Event Identification** Events • Influencing Factors • Event Identification Techniques Event Interdependencies • Event Categories Distinguishing Risk and Opportunities	• Common risk language and definitions • Common process classification scheme • Documented interdependencies
Infrastructure components for executing selected risk responses: • Written policies for executing selected risk responses • Processes and procedures • People and structure – assigned risk and process owners	**Risk Assessment** Inherent and Residual Risk • Establishing Likelihood and Impact Data Sources • Assessment Techniques • Event Relationships	• Unacceptable gaps in capabilities around managing priority risks • Assessment of options
	Risk Response Evaluating Possible Risk Responses • Selected Responses Portfolio View	• Selected risk management responses • Integration of selected risk responses with overall strategy and business plans • Portfolio view of residual risk
	Control Activities Integration with Risk Response • Types of Control Activities Policies and Procedures • Controls over Information Systems Entity-Specific	
• Balanced scorecard components • Key metrics • Results of internal audits • Risk management improvement action plan status to close unacceptable gaps • Actual risk incidents or near misses • Best practices information	**Information and Communication** Information • Communication	Infrastructure components for executing selected risk responses: • Management reports, including pending improvement action plans • Methodologies, i.e., risk measurement methodologies, models and assumptions • Systems and data
	Monitoring Ongoing Monitoring Activities • Separate Evaluations Reporting Deficiencies	

Source: The above summary of attributes by component is from *Application Techniques of COSO ERM Framework*

Illustrated Focus of Data Elements

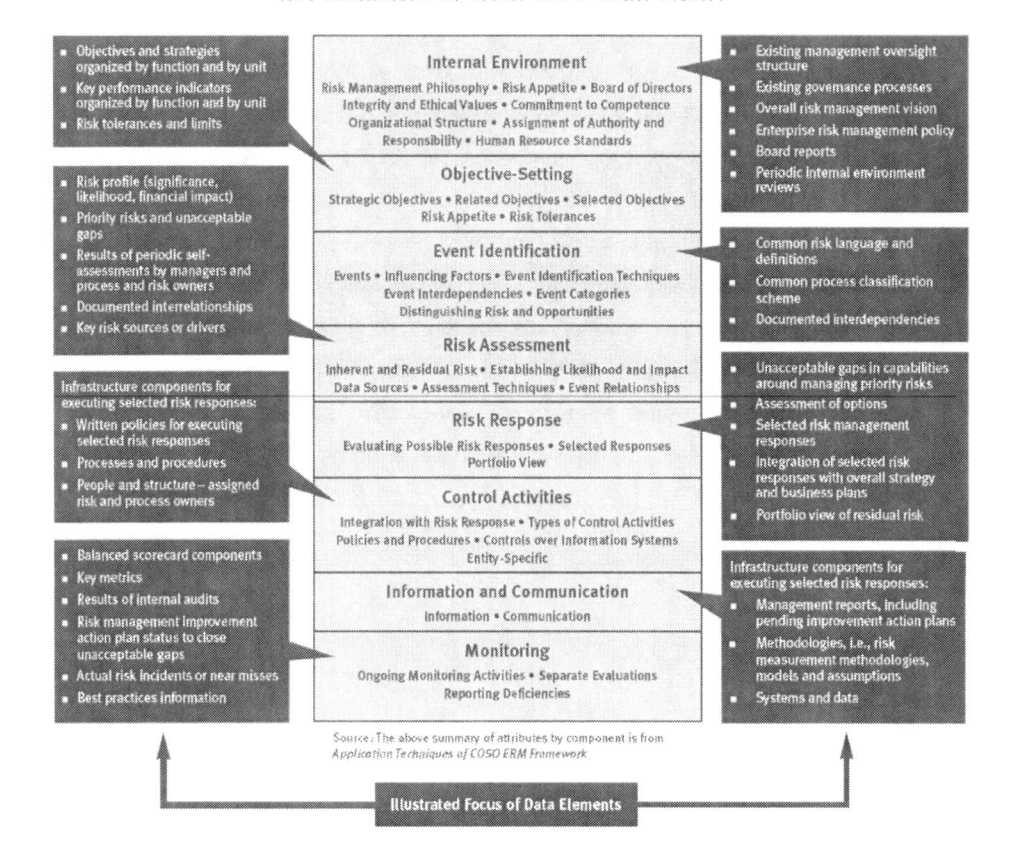

Figure-3. COSO Enterprise Risk Management Basic Framework (COSO, 2004).

Internal Environment
Risk Management Philosophy – Risk Appetite – Board of Directors – Integrity and Ethical Values – Commitment to Competence – Organizational Structure – Assignment of Authority and Responsibility – Human Resource Standards

Objective Setting
Strategic Objectives – Related Objectives – Selected Objectives – Risk Appetite – Risk Tolerances

Event Identification
Events – Influencing Factors – Event Identification Techniques – Event Interdependencies – Event Categories – Distinguishing Risks and Opportunities

Risk Assessment
Inherent and Residual Risk – Establishing Likelihood and Impact – Data Sources – Assessment Techniques – Event Relationships

Risk Response
Evaluating Possible Responses – Selected Responses – Portfolio View

Control Activities
Integration with Risk Response – Types of Control Activities – Policies and Procedures – Controls Over Information Systems – Entity Specific

Information and Communication
Information – Communication

Monitoring
Ongoing Monitoring Activities – Separate Evaluations – Reporting Deficiencies

Figure-4. COSO Enterprise Risk Components (COSO, Enterprise Risk Management—Integrated Framework: Application Techniques, 2004:2.).

The COSO "Enterprise Risk Management-Integrated Framework" published in 2004 defines ERM as: "A process, effected by an entity's board of directors, management, and other personnel, applied in strategy setting and across the enterprise, designed to identify potential events that may affect the entity, and manage risk to be within its risk appetite, to provide reasonable assurance regarding the achievement of entity objectives."

The COSO ERM Framework has an eight component and four objectives categories. It is an expansion of the COSO Internal Control - Integrated Framework published in 1992 and amended in 1994. The eight components - additional components highlighted - are:

- Internal Environment
- Objective setting
- Event Identification
- Risk assessment
- Risk response
- Control activities
- Information and communication
- Monitoring

The four objectives categories - additional components highlighted - are:

- Strategy - high level goals: aligned the organizations mission.
- Operations - effective and efficient use of resources
- Financial Reporting - reliability of operational and financial reporting
- Compliance - compliance with applicable laws and regulations.

Oliver Wyman ERM framework is consisting of four main parts. They are:

- ERM infrastructure
- ERM Process
- ERM Integration
- ERM culture and enabling activities.

Oliver Wyman's framework is based on COSO framework. Related efforts are integrated with COSO framework.

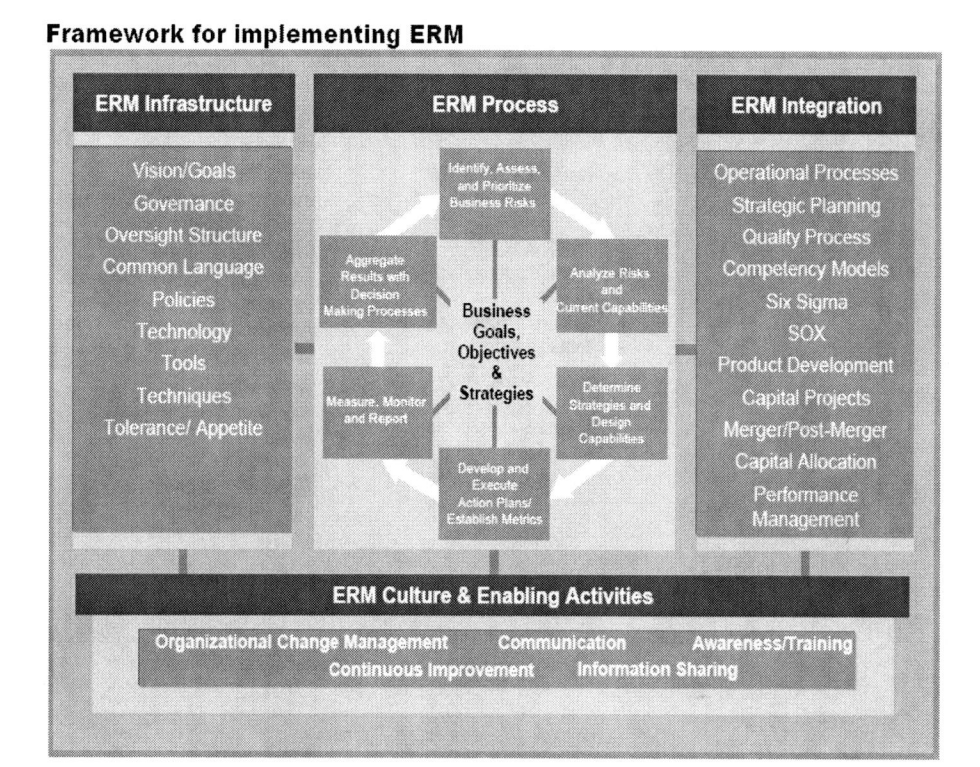

Framework for implementing ERM

ERM Infrastructure	ERM Process	ERM Integration
Vision/Goals Governance Oversight Structure Common Language Policies Technology Tools Techniques Tolerance/ Appetite	Identify, Assess, and Prioritize Business Risks Aggregate Results with Decision Making Processes Analyze Risks and Current Capabilities Business Goals, Objectives & Strategies Measure, Monitor and Report Determine Strategies and Design Capabilities Develop and Execute Action Plans/ Establish Metrics	Operational Processes Strategic Planning Quality Process Competency Models Six Sigma SOX Product Development Capital Projects Merger/Post-Merger Capital Allocation Performance Management

ERM Culture & Enabling Activities

Organizational Change Management Communication Awareness/Training
Continuous Improvement Information Sharing

Source: Mercer Oliver Wyman 2005

ERM Infrastructure

ERM Infrastructure
- Vision/Goals
- Governance
- Oversight Structure
- Common Language
- Policies
- Technology
- Tools
- Techniques
- Tolerance/ Appetite

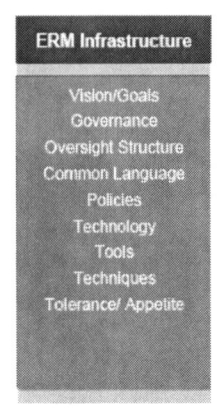

Objective: Network of organizational and governance tools/ components to support the ERM Process and integration.

Vision/Goals
- Mission statement
- Value Proposition and Benefits statement

Governance/Oversight
- Organizational accountabilities and responsibilities
- Oversight structure/span of control
- Roles and responsibilities
- Monitoring

Common Language
- Company-wide understanding of risk terminology
- Business Risk Inventory

Policies & Procedures
- Risk policy manuals
- Standard operating procedures

Technology & Tools
- Risk management databases
- Analytical applications

Tools/ Techniques
- Risk diagnostic tools
- Measurement
- Modeling
- Casual Analysis

Tolerances/Limits
- Matrix of tolerances and limits
- Process for defining tolerance/ appetite

Objective: Methodology to identify, assess, prioritize, manage, and aggregate risk exposures and opportunities across the enterprise.

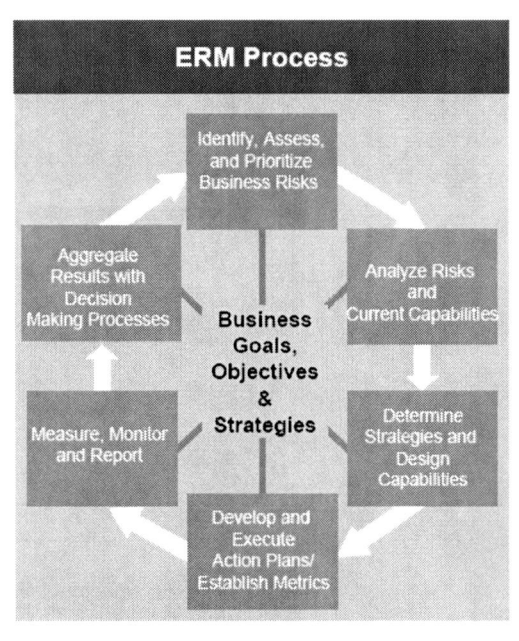

ERM Process

- Identify, Assess, and Prioritize Business Risks
- Analyze Risks and Current Capabilities
- Determine Strategies and Design Capabilities
- Develop and Execute Action Plans/ Establish Metrics
- Measure, Monitor and Report
- Aggregate Results with Decision Making Processes

Business Goals, Objectives & Strategies

- Formal & continuous
- Align risks with goals and objectives
- Identify, assess, and prioritize risks
- Analyze risks (root cause, impact, interrelationships, and capabilities)
  - Identify gaps in management of risks
  - Develop and determine risk strategies
  - Execute risk mitigation plans
  - Create risk metrics
  - Monitor and report on current status

Objective: Organizational behavior reinforcing the ERM structure.

- Supports other aspects of ERM Framework through enabling activities:
  - Awareness/ Training
  - Communication
  - Continuous improvement
  - Information Sharing
  - Performance Management and Rewords
  - Organizational Change Management
  - Voice of the Employee

ERM Culture & Enabling Activities
Organizational Change Management   Communication   Awareness/Training
Continuous Improvement   Information Sharing

Source: Mercer Oliver Wyman 2005.

2.6. The Institute of Management Accountants' (IMA) "A Global Perspective on Assessing Internal Control over Financial Reporting" (ICoFR)

IMA developed a risk-based framework to assist company management in more cost effective compliance with SOX 404 requirements. Titled "A Global Perspective on Assessing Internal Control over Financial Reporting" (ICoFR), it includes self assessments by CFOs and business process owners. The framework has been marketing tested and draws on advances in global risk and quality management disciplines over many years. Some members of the business community have noted that SOX 404 requirements have resulted in smaller publicly traded companies delisting or threatening to delist; larger corporations employing full-time staffs and expensive consultants and not realizing the value in their compliance programs; Furthermore, an erosion of U.S. global competitiveness. IMA developed the framework and delivered it to the SEC in order to provide considered leadership as the SEC develops its own version of management assessment guidance, which many hope will address the implementation issues associated with SOX 404 compliances in the more than three years since the Sarbanes-Oxley Act was passed. ICoFR heavily relies on advances in global risk management, including how to "treat" risks once an "assurance context" has been established with appropriate business objectives. The assurance context as it relates to SOX 404 is materially fault-free financial statements enabled by an effective system of internal controls. The risk based framework works equally well with other business contexts/applications, however, such as business continuity planning, operations management, and cost optimization. The ICoFR framework also relies on traditional Total Quality Management (TQM) principles. For example, once the assurance context has been established and the initial control portfolio is selected to address "threats to achievement" of objectives, the residual risk that remains is quantifiable (e.g., by analysis of historical error rates) and tested against pre established bounds. This gradually assists to determine if the risk is acceptable or not.

2.7. Basel II

The Basel Committee on Banking Supervision updated its original Basel Accord with Basel II and its related new framework. The framework is designed to improve the international banking system and make it stronger. The framework is focused on maintaining consistent capital adequacy requirements among banks. A key idea behind the framework is that banks should match capital to the actual level of risks and to set minimum capital levels. The framework applies to "internationally active banks" and has three pillars: minimum capital requirements, supervisory review, and market discipline.

2.8. Standard & Poor's and Enterprise Risk Management (ERM)

Standard & Poor's (S&P) has already started to incorporate a company's ERM practice into the S&P rating of the company. S&P currently applies this rating to both financial institutions and insurers. Its framework for evaluating ERM at banks includes a review of ERM policies, ERM infrastructure, and ERM methodology. ERM policies should address risk culture, appetite, and strategy; control and monitoring; in addition, disclosure and awareness. ERM infrastructure covers risk technology, operations, and risk training. ERM methodology refers to capital allocation, model vetting, and valuation methods. The framework for evaluating insurers includes an assessment of risk management culture, risk controls, emerging risk management, risk and capital models, and strategic risk management. Standard and Poor's has stated that the insurer is rated weak, adequate, strong, or excellent. An adequate rating would mean an insurer has "fully functioning as risk control systems in place for all major risks."

2.9. RIMS Risk Maturity Model for Enterprise Risk Management

ERM as defined by the Risk and Insurance Management Society (RIMS) is the culture, processes and tools to identify strategic opportunities and reduce uncertainty. ERM is a comprehensive view of risk from both operational and strategic perspectives and is a process that suffers the reduction of uncertainty and promotes the exploitation of opportunities.

According to the RIMS Risk Maturity Model for ERM, the following seven core competencies, or attributes, measure how well enterprise risk management is embraced by management and ingrained within the organization. A maturity level is determined for each attribute and ERM maturity is determined by the weakest link.

1. ERM-based approach - Degree of executive support for an ERM-based approach within the corporate culture. This goes beyond regulatory compliance across all processes, functions, business lines, roles and geographies. Degree of integration, communication and coordination of internal audit, information technology, compliance, control and risk management.

2. ERM process management - Degree of weaving the ERM Process into business processes and using ERM Process steps to identify, assess, evaluate, mitigate and monitor. Degree of incorporating qualitative methods supported by quantitative methods, analysis, tools and models.

3. Risk appetite management – Degree of understanding the risk-reward tradeoffs within the business. Accountability within leadership and policy to guide decision-making and attack gaps between perceived and actual risk. Risk appetite clearly sets the limit of acceptable risk and risk tolerance defines the variation of measuring risk appetite that management deems acceptable.

4. Root cause discipline - Degree of discipline applied to measuring a problem's root cause and binding events with their process sources to drive the reduction of uncertainty, collection of information and measurement of the controls' effectiveness. The degree of risk from people, external environment, systems, processes and relationships is explored.

5. Uncovering risks - Degree of quality and penetration coverage of risk assessment activities in documenting risks and opportunities. Degree of collecting knowledge from employee expertise, databases and other electronic files (such as Microsoft® Word, Excel®, etc) to uncover dependencies and correlation across the enterprise.

6. Performance management - Degree of executing vision and strategy, working from financial, customer, business process and learning and growth perspectives, such as Kaplan's balanced scorecard, or similar approach. Degree of exposure to uncertainty, or potential deviations from plans or expectations.

7. Business resiliency and sustainability – Extent to which the ERM Process's sustainability aspects are integrated into operational planning. This includes evaluating how planning supports resiliency and value. The degree of ownership and planning beyond recovering technology platforms. Examples include vendor and distribution dependencies, supply chain disruptions, dramatic market pricing changes, cash flow volatility, business liquidity, etc.

2.10. AIRMIC

This Risk Management Standard is the result of work by a team drawn from the major risk management organisations in the UK - The Institute of Risk Management (IRM), The Association of Insurance and Risk Managers (AIRMIC) and ALARM The National Forum for Risk Management in the Public Sector. In addition, the team sought the views and opinions of a wide range of other professional bodies with interests in risk management, during an extensive period of consultation. Risk management is a rapidly developing discipline and there are many and varied views and descriptions of what risk management involves, how it should be conducted, and what it is for. Some form of standard is needed to ensure that there is an agreed:

- Terminology related to the words used.
- Process by which risk management can be carried out.
- Organization structure for risk management.
- Objective for risk management.

Importantly, the standard recognises that risk has both an upside and a downside. Risk management is not just something for corporations or public organisations, but for any activity whether short or long term. The benefits and opportunities should be viewed not just in the context of the activity itself but in relation to the many and varied stakeholders who can be affected. There are many ways of achieving the objectives of risk management, and it would be impossible to try to set them complete in a single document. Therefore, it was never intended to produce a prescriptive Standard which would have led to a box ticking approach to establish a certifiable process. By meeting the various component parts of this standard, albeit in different ways, organizations will be in a position to report that they are in compliance. The standard represents best practice against which organizations can measure themselves.

Figure-5 shows the 2002 business based risk management framework, a joint venture by the Institute of Risk Management, The Association of Insurance and Risk Managers, and the National Forum for Risk Management in the Public Sector, which are all based in the UK. The standard is available at http://www.airmic.com/.

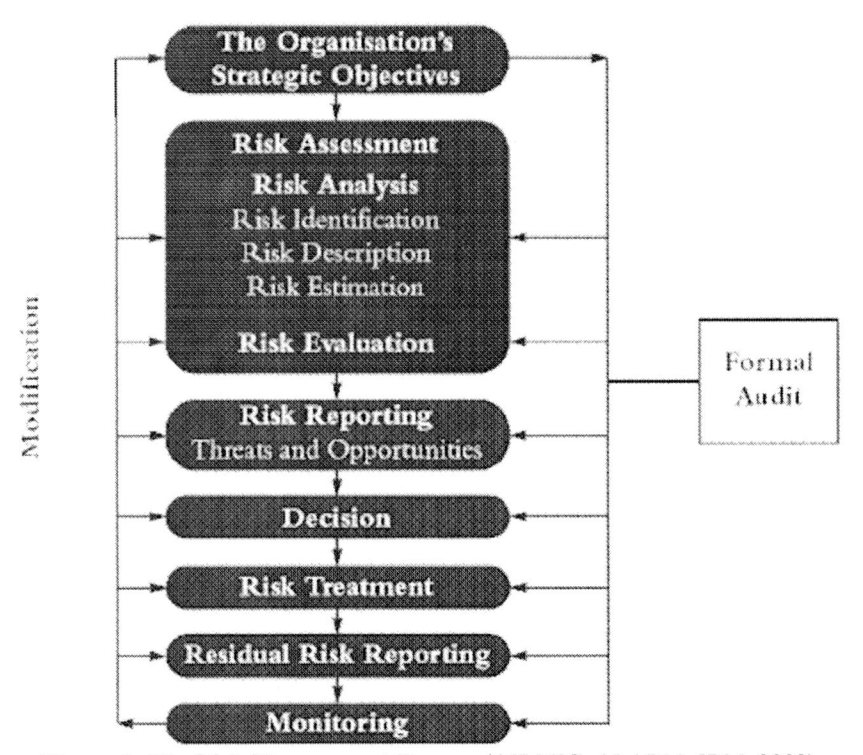

Figure-5: The Risk Management Process (AIRMIC, ALARM, IRM, 2002)

2.11. An overview comparison of the AIRMIC/ALARM/ IRM Risk Management Standard with: The Australia /New Zealand Standard AS/NZS 4360:2004 and The COSO Enterprise Risk Management - Integrated Framework

The Risk Management Standard developed by AIRMIC, IRM and ALARM has been compared with the Australia / New Zealand Standard (AS/NZS 4360:2004 and the COSO Enterprise Risk Management - Integrated Framework. The comparison is set out in the tabular format with a summary of key points complied by more detailed comments on each main section of the Standards and how they compare. At a high level, all three documents are similar in that each them:

-sets out a generic process for risk management and accepts that there needs to be flexibility in implementation is applicable to a wide range of professional systems and activities recognizes that management of risk is part of good management practice, should be continuous and is best embedded into existing practices / business processes.

- recognises that there can be positive outcomes as well as negative outcomes sets out steps in the risk management process with brief guidance on each. (In the case of the Australia/ New Zealand and COSO documents, a second volume provides much more detailed guidance on the implementation of each step.) defines the terminology used The comparison table takes each main element of the AIRMIC/IRM/ALARM Standard and comments on the comparable section in the other documents or how a particular topic is addressed if there is no exactly comparable section. It also comments on additional material in the more detailed AS/NZS and COSO documents which is not part of the AIRMIC/IRM/ALARM Standard.

All three standards provide useful frameworks for risk management and guidance on implementation. Those familiar with the AIRMIC/IRM/ALARM Standard or applying it for the first time, may find it helpful also to refer to the other documents for additional information or a different perspective on a particular aspect of the risk management process.

In the following sections, indicated some of the material in the AS/NZS and COSO documents that adds to the AIRMIC/IRM/ALARM Standard and may be helpful in developing a comprehensive approach to risk management.

Business Objectives and Objective Setting

The AIRMIC/IRM/ALARM standard is emphasis the importance of relating risk management to strategic and operational objectives of organizations and the threats / opportunities related to achieving those objectives. AS/NZS states that the first step in establishing the context within which an organisation goes is to establish the organisation s objectives and the internal and external environment in which the objectives are pursued. COSO includes objective setting as one key component of its risk management process, making it clear that objective setting is a precondition to event identification, risk assessment and risk response. There must first be objectives before management can identify and assess risks to their achievement and necessary actions to manage the risks. It identifies four key categories of objectives:

- Strategic and the high level goals, aligned with supporting the organisation s vision. These reflect management's choice as to how the organisation will take to create value for stakeholders.

- Operations the objectives relating to the effectiveness and efficiency of the organisation s operations, including performance / profitability goals and safeguarding against loss.

- Reporting the objectives relating to achieving reliable reporting both internal and external to the organisation.

- Compliance the objectives relating to meeting the demands of relevant laws and regulations. These requirements may relate to trade, pricing, taxes, environment, employee welfare, etc., and an organisation's compliance record can have a significant effect on its reputation.

COSO refers to the operations, reporting and compliance objectives as related objectives as they support and are aligned to the strategy of the organisation. It also points out that objectives in one category my overlap with or support objectives in another category.

COSO also draws a distinction between objectives whose achievement is not solely under the organisation s control and those where the organisation has control over its ability to do what is needed. Achievement of strategic and operations objectives may be influenced by external factors/ events whereas achieving compliance and reporting objectives is largely within the organisation's control.

In the Application Techniques document, COSO gives further guidance on setting strategic objectives and the use of risk assessment, at this stage, to gradually assist to decide between different options. It presents illustrations of linkages between the organisation mission / vision and its strategic and related objectives.There is also a useful section on risk appetite with questions that management might ask when considering risk appetite.

Risk Assessment

The AIRMIC/IRM/ALARM standard establishes that the estimation of probability of occurrence and the possible consequences can be qualitative, semi quantitative or quantitative. It gives simple examples relating both to threats and opportunities. AS/NZS expands on this and provides a list of pertinent information sources and techniques which can be used when assessing probability of occurrence and consequences. In the Guidelines Document AS/NZS provides much more information on the following:

- The choice of analysis method, which will be influenced by the context, the objectives and the resources that can be applied to the analysis.

- Types of risk measurement scales are discussed and examples of graphical representation of likelihood and consequence are given.

- Consequence and likelihood tables. These express different levels of severity for different types of consequence such as profit reduction, environmental impact, reputation impact, legal/regulatory impact, etc. Tables of likelihood also illustrate different levels of likelihood in terms of frequencies and simply in descriptive terms.

The level of risk: AS/NZS shows how the degree of risk can be described, depending on the type of analysis that has been undertaken. How opportunities can be analysed. Different levels of opportunity and how these can be presented are shown. Key questions may be asked when analysing risks. COSO provides expands methodology for assessing risks both qualitatively and quantitatively. In the Application Techniques document COSO offers a useful description of how value at risk models can be used, using illustrations of market value at risk, cash flow at risk, earnings at risk, etc. It also addresses sensitivity analysis and scenario analysis.

COSO offers examples of different ways of portraying risk assessment results including, risk maps, risk matrices using mean values of likelihood and impact, and risk matrices showing the variability in likelihood and impact.

The AIRMIC/IRM/ALARM standard indicates that risk treatment includes control / mitigation as a major element, but also extends to risk avoidance, risk transfer, risk financing, etc. It also stresses the need to evaluate the cost effectiveness of any proposed risk treatment measures.

AS/NZS provides more detail and deals separately with options for treatment of risks with positive outcomes versus treatment of risks with negative outcomes. It identifies options for treatment of risks with positive outcomes as including:

- Actively seeking an opportunity by deciding to start or continue an activity which is likely to create the opportunity.

- Changing the likelihood of the opportunity

- Changing the outcomes to increase the extent of the profits

- Sharing the opportunity with other parties in order to increase the likelihood and / or the gain.

- Retaining the opportunity without any immediate action being required.

In the case of risks with negative outcomes, AS/NZS identifies similar types of treatment options as follows: -

- Avoiding the risk by deciding not to start or continue with an activity.

- Changing the likelihood of negative outcomes

- Changing the results to reduce the extent of losses.

- Sharing the risk via contracts, insurance, etc., in order to transfer liability

- Retaining the risk.

In the Guidelines document AS/NZS provides more information on treatment options including crisis/ business continuity plans, contracting and insurance.It sets out guidance on designing risk treatment options and the trade- off between costs and benefits. It describes a qualitative approach to cost benefit analysis as well as a quantitative approach. Finally, it stresses the importance of risk treatment plans which should:

-Identify responsibilities, schedules, budgets, performance measures and expected outcomes of risk treatment.

- Include mechanisms for assessing and monitoring treatment effectiveness against treatment objectives

- Document how the chosen options will be implemented.

In its section on risk response, COSO introduces the portfolio, or entity wide, perspective of risk. For example, the risks in different business units of a major company may be within the risk tolerance levels of those business units, but taken together, these risks may exceed the risk appetite of the company as a whole. In the Application Techniques, COSO gives further detail on:

-Linking risk response to objectives, events and risk assessment

- The effect of risk response on residual risk

- Multiple risk responses

- Cost benefit analysis of alternative risk response

- Further information on the portfolio view of residual risk

COSO contains a section on the limitations of ERM. It points out that no matter how well designed and implemented, ERM may only provide reasonable assurance to the management and the Board of Directors that the organisation's objectives will be achieved.

It identifies three important issues that need to be recognised:

- Risk relates to the future which is inherently uncertain Enterprise risk management, however effective, operates at different levels with respect to different objectives. It can serve to ensure that management is aware of the extent to which the organisation is moving toward achievement of its objectives. It cannot provide assurance that the objectives will be achieved. Enterprise risk management cannot provide absolute assurance with respect to any of the assurance categories. The section identifies ways in which a well designed risk management system can break down which include human judgment, human errors caused by carelessness, distraction or fatigue, collusion between two or more individuals and the deliberate over riding of policies / procedures by management. Following the table is given an overview comparison of this three ERM standard and its frameworks (AIRMIC 2005).

Table: An overview comparison of the AIRMIC/ALARM/ IRM Risk Management Standard with the Australia /New Zealand Standard and the COSO Enterprise Risk Management - Integrated Framework (Source: AIRMIC 2005)

A Risk Management Standard AIRMIC / ALARM / IRM 2002	Australian/New Zealand Standard AS/NZS 4360: 2004	Enterprise Risk Management Integrated Framework COSO 2004
Summary A short 14-page document which sets out the "standard" with the terminology definitions as an appendix.	**Summary** A 30 page document setting out the standard with a companion volume (109 pages) setting out Risk Management Guidelines.	**Summary** A 125-page document sets out an executive summary (7pages) follow by a detailed description of the Risk Management Framework.

Sets out a generic process for risk management, applicable to a wide range of organizations / activities. Recognizes there is an upside to risk as well as a "downside", but addresses mainly the downside. Sets out steps in the risk management process with very brief guidance on each. Follows the terminology for risk, set out in the ISO/IEC Guide 73 Risk Management Vocabulary- Guidelines for use in Standards.	The most recent of the three documents. Standard sets out a generic process for risk management which is independent of any specific industry or economic sector. Recognizes "upside" and "downside" of risk, referring to potential gains and potential losses and to "positive and negative outcomes". Addresses both, in parts of the standard e.g. Risk Treatment. Sets out process and brief content for each step. The process is very similar to that in the AIRMIC Standard. Provides its own definitions of terms with reference to ISO definitions in some cases. Companion volume Risk Management Guidelines. Reproduces each section of the Standard and then expands on it with detailed guidance and examples.	A second volume (105 pages) provides "Application Techniques" with detailed guidance and examples. Sets out a generic risk management process with more emphasis on "business risk", value creation and internal control. Recognizes "upside" and "downside" of risk, expressing this more in terms of uncertainty and the associated risks and opportunities. Sets out components of risk management, i.e. the risk management process. Presents a three dimensional matrix to relate the organizations objectives to the risk management components and to the business unit structure of the organization. Provides a section on "definition" which contains significant discussion as well as defining key terms, such as enterprise risk management. It does not set out definitions of each term in the same way as the other two. Companion volume Application Techniques. Takes each component of risk management and gives detailed guidance and examples on how to implement each.
Introduction Makes the point that standard is needed to ensure an agreed: -<ul><li>use of terminology</li><li>process by which risk management is carried out</li><li>organization structure for risk management</li><li>objective for risk management</li></ul>Establishes that standard is	**Preface and Foreword** Comparable to AIRMIC introduction and COSO Foreword. Only document that is a revision of an earlier Standard (1995 and revised 1999) Intention is to provide generic framework with more emphasis on: -<ul><li>embedding risk management practices in an organizations culture</li><li>Risk as an exposure to the</li></ul>	**Foreword** Comparable to AIRMIC Introduction. Refers to earlier document; Internal Control- Integrated Framework. Expresses the need for an enterprise risk management framework: -<ul><li>providing key principles/concepts</li><li>a common language</li><li>clear direction and guidance</li></ul>Expands on, but does not replace, the earlier internal control document

not prescriptive and that there is flexibility in meeting the component parts. Standard represents best practice against which organizations can measure themselves.	consequences of uncertainty and potential deviations from what is planned/expected. ■ Managing potential gains as well as potential losses. ■ Guidance and examples provided in a new handbook.	which is incorporated in this wider enterprise risk management framework. Organizations can use this framewo to move to a fuller risk management process.
Risk Standard defines risk (as per ISO/IEC guide 73) Definition of all other terms is in the reproduction of ISO/IEC Guide 73 in the Appendix. Emphasizes opportunities for benefit (upside) as well as threats to success (downside) Makes the point that safety risk is concerned only with the negative.	**Scope and General** AS/NZS defines risk in this section and also sets out all other definitions of terms. Definitions are AS/NZS own definitions with use of ISO terminology in some cases. Scope and general also has some further introduction setting out the objective of the standard and that it is not intended to enforce uniformity of risk management systems.	**Definition** The first main section in the framework document has substantia discussion of the key terms. Risk is defined as possibility of an event that will have an adverse effec on achieving objectives. Opportunit is defined as possibility of an event that will positively affect achieveme of objectives.
Risk Management Standard emphasizes risk management as: - ■ central part of strategic management ■ a continuous and developing process ■ part the culture of the organization ■ supporting operational efficiency at all levels Standard describes external and internal drivers of risk, categorizing them as financial, strategic, hazard and operational. Standard sets out the basic risk management process diagram. Standard sets out benefits of risk management.	**Risk management process overview and Risk Management Context** Basic risk management process diagram is set out. This is very similar to the process set out in the AIRMIC standard. The context includes the organization's internal and external environment and the interface between the two. The same concept as expressed in the AIRMIC diagram of external and internal drivers of risk and the interface between the two.	**Components of Risk Management** COSO does not have an exactly comparable section here, but discusses in a number of places: - The link to business objectives The organization's internal environment Four categories of objectives strategic, operations, reporting and compliance Risk management philosophy and risk appetite.
Objective Setting There is no specific section dealing with objective	**Objectives** Goals and objectives are	**Objective setting** COSO has objective setting as one component of risk management.

setting (as in COSO), but AIRMIC does stress the importance of relating risk management and risk assessment to strategic objectives.	addressed as part of establishing the risk management context.	It emphasizes strategic objectives as supporting the organizations vision and mission. Categories of related objectives are identified as Operations, Reporting and Compliance. This section also addresses achievement of objectives, risk appetite and risk tolerance of the organization.
Risk Identification AIRMIC treats risk identification as part of risk analysis which also includes risk description and risk estimation. Guidance is very limited risk identification should be done in a methodical way to ensure that all activities and all risks are defined. A short list of risk identification techniques is given in the appendix.	**Identify Risks** Very short section in which AS/NZS stresses need for systematic approach to identify risks, whether or not they are under the control of the organization. The Risk Management Guidelines expand on the identification process, the information needed, the approaches to identifying risks and documentation of risk identification.	**Event Identification** COSO refers to "events" (external or internal) which affect implementation of strategy. Events may have positive or negative impact. Document lists external and internal influencing factors that drive events and event categories. (This appears comparable to the AIRMIC diagram of Drivers of Key Risks.) COSO gives more detail on event identification techniques in the framework document. The Application Techniques document provides a variety of examples with outlines for facilitated workshops, process flow analysis, questionnaires, etc.
Risk Description Deals briefly with structured format for recording the risks identified (with an example table)	**Documentation** Deals with recording the risk identification step (in the Guidelines) and gives examples of risk registers in Section 10 of the Guidelines Recording the Risk Management Process.	**Risk Description** COSO does not deal separately with recording risk identification, but incorporates it into the recording of risk assessment.
Risk Assessment AIRMIC uses ISO term risk estimation. Gives simple tables of examples for assessing consequences and probability for both threats and opportunities.	**Analyze Risks** AS/NZS addresses qualitative, semi quantitative and quantitative estimation of consequences and likelihood. (and the need to take account of existing controls) It lists information sources and techniques for estimating consequences and likelihood.	**Risk Assessment** No significant differences from the other documents. COSO addresses inherent and residual risk. COSO discusses assessment techniques such as benchmarking, probabilistic and non-probabilistic methods. The Risk assessment section in the Application Techniques document is

	The Risk Assessment section of the Guidelines document is comprehensive. It shows a good spread of risk assessment approaches from the very simple to the more detailed quantitative. It also specifically addresses the analysis of opportunities.	comprehensive. It tends to be more financially oriented with analyses of earnings at risk, cash flow at risk, value at risk, etc.
Risk Evaluation Very short section makes the point that after risk assessment, it is necessary to compare risks to risk criteria established by the organization. Decisions about accepting or treating a risk should then be made.	**Risk Evaluation** AS/NZS has similar very short section. The Guidelines cover evaluation criteria, the concepts of tolerable risk and ALARP. There is also reference to historical events in determining risk criteria.	**Risk Evaluation** No exactly comparable section. Some comments are incorporated in the Risk Assessment and Risk Response Sections.
Risk Reporting and Communication AIRMIC deals with reporting of risks internally and externally, before moving on to risk treatment.	**Risk Reporting and Communication** AS/NZS deals with communication and consultation separately at the start of the standard.	**Risk Reporting and Communication** COSO addresses information and communication after Risk Response and Control Activities.
Risk Treatment AIRMIC does not give much detail, but states that risk control/ mitigation is a major element of risk treatment which also extends to avoidance, risk transfer and risk financing. It addresses cost/effectiveness of risk treatment and that compliance with laws and regulations is not optional.	**Treat Risks** AS/NZS deals separately with options for treating risks with positive outcomes and for those with negative outcomes. It briefly refers to the cost / benefit analysis of treatment options. The Guidelines provide more information on treatment options, including sharing risk, contracting, insurance, contingency planning, etc. Guidelines also deal with selecting treatment options and cost / benefit analysis both qualitative and quantitative.	**Risk Response** COSO deals with treatment options four categories: - Avoidance, Reduction, Sharing and Acceptance Framework document deals very briefly with cost / benefit analysis. The Applications techniques document provides more detail on risk responses and gives examples of tables recording actions, risk reduction, etc.
Monitoring and Review of Risk Management AIRMIC makes the point	**Monitor and Review** AS/ANZ indicates that ongoing review is essential and that	**Monitoring** COSO separates monitoring into

that monitoring should provide assurance that risks are identified and appropriate controls are in place.	lessons should be learned by reviewing events, treatment plans and their outcomes. Guidelines expand on this, dealing with assurance and monitoring, risk management performance measurement and post-event analysis.	ongoing monitoring activities and separate evaluations. It deals with reporting in this section including what is reported and to whom.
Structure and Administration of Risk Management The standard sets out roles and responsibilities for: - <ul><li>The Board</li><li>Business units</li><li>The Risk management Function</li><li>Internal Audit</li></ul> In addition it comments on Risk Management Policy and resources for Implementation. **(No equivalent to COSO Section)**	**Establishing effective Risk Management** AS/ANZ deals more generally with this area and refers to: - <ul><li>evaluating existing practices</li><li>Ensuring senior management support</li><li>Establishing accountability and authority</li><li>Ensuring adequate resources</li></ul> The Guidelines expand on this to some extent, but not significantly. **(No equivalent to COSO Section)**	**Roles and Responsibilities.** COSO sets out roles and responsibilities for: - <ul><li>The Board</li><li>Management</li><li>The Risk Officer</li><li>Financial Executives</li><li>Internal auditors</li><li>External parties</li></ul> The Application Techniques provide more detail including example role descriptions for the Chief Risk Officer, the CEO, the Audit Committee, the Risk Committee, etc. **Limitations of Enterprise Risk Management** COSO indicates that however good the risk management system, it can only provide reasonable assurance regarding achievement of objectives. Limitations include: - <ul><li>Management processes</li><li>Human error/ mistakes</li><li>Deliberate circumventing of controls</li><li>Costs of risk responses</li><li>Etc.</li></ul>

Source: AIRMIC, 2005.

2.12. Transport Canada

Figure-6 illustrates the Canadian Risk Management Standard (Guide) Q850 (CSA, 1997). It is a generic standard and was the first to formally introduce the themes of:

1. Explicit decision-making at most steps in the process, including the decision option of "end" consideration of a risk.

2. *Stakeholders*, stakeholder analysis, and introduction of stakeholder needs, issues, and concerns in the *risk evaluation*, etc.

3. Explicit introduction of *risk communication* at each functional step in the framework.

4. Initiation step where the technical and administrative risk management "process" is designed and resourced. Initiation is a function in the organization's risk management system.

5. Preliminary Analysis, which is a screening level risk analysis and *risk evaluation* (both together are called *risk assessment*). This is illustrated in the benchmark framework (Figure- 2).

6. Documentation needs and the creation of a "risk library" for any application of the process.

This standard was a milestone and the Australian-New Zealand standard issued in 1995 was revised in 1999 to incorporate some of these ideas and extend them in terms of the concept of "Context" and other innovations. The Canadian standard in Figure 4 now has some non-standard (ISO) terminology, for example, *Risk Control* is now *Risk Treatment* after implementation, and *Risk Treatment* is the process of finding a treatment to modify the risk that the decision-makers deem acceptable. However, most of the terminology is similar to ISO/IEC Guide 73.

The role of the decision-maker is shown at 4 points in the framework, after the completion of major functional processes, such as *risk estimation, risk evaluation* and *risk treatment* (shown as *risk control*). Between preliminary analysis and *risk estimation,* there is a decision as to which of the many risks identified (and given a preliminary assessment) are priority risks which need further attention. Figure-6 illustrates this for the benchmark framework.

Dr. Ayse KUCUK YILMAZ

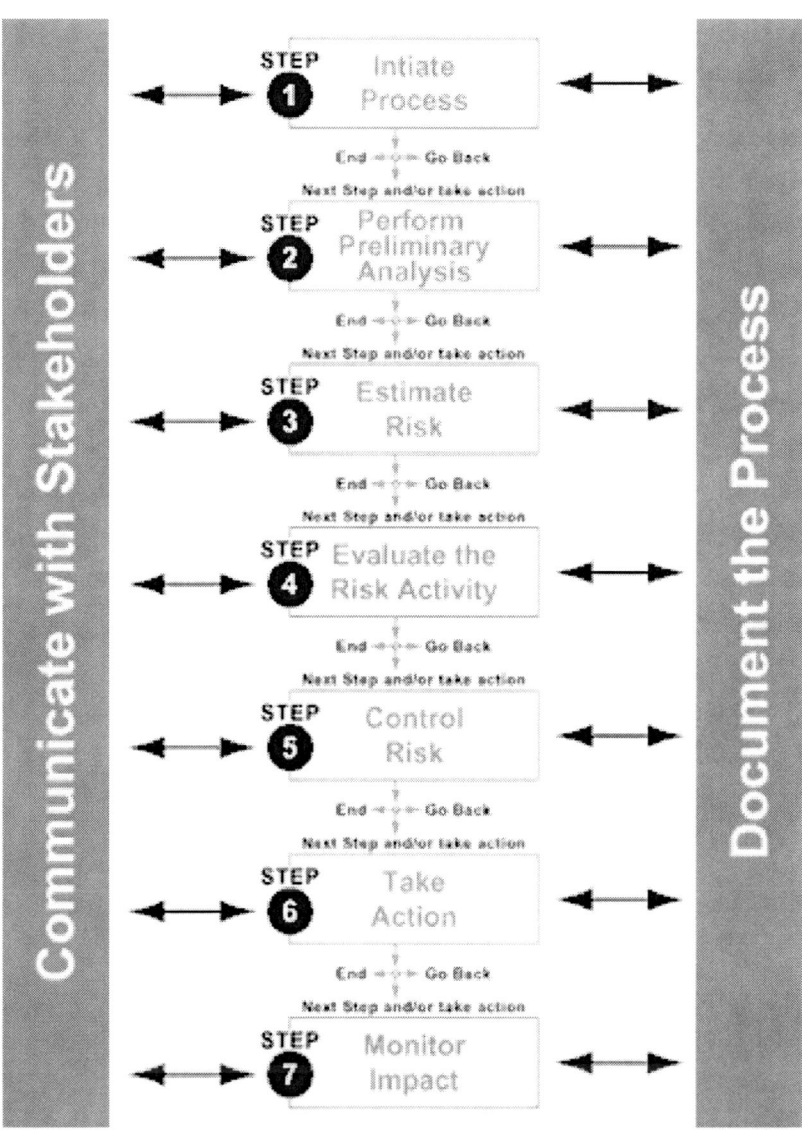

Figure-6. Steps in the Q850 Risk Management Decision-Making Process - Detailed Model (Transport Canada, The Seven-Step Risk Management Process, http://www.tc.gc.ca/civilaviation/systemsafety/pubs/tp13095/Q850/what.htm, 2007).

2.13. Japaneese Industrial Risk Management Standard

Japan issued standard "JSI Q 2001:2001 – Guidelines for development and implementation of *risk management system*", using the ISO terminology for the risk management system as well as other terms. Figure-7 shows the concept of the risk management system as an integral part of an organization's structure established to maintain risk management activities and the associated system that carries out those activities. The standard is compatible with the benchmark framework. There are two basic advances in the standard, the first is the formal definition and development of the risk management system (in contrast to the usual development of the risk management framework) and the second advance is the linkage of the risk management system directly to Total Quality Management concepts, including continuous improvement. In the details of the standard, there is a focus on prevention of the events following the 1995 major earthquake when some 5,000 firms and organizations were unable to quickly restart operations.

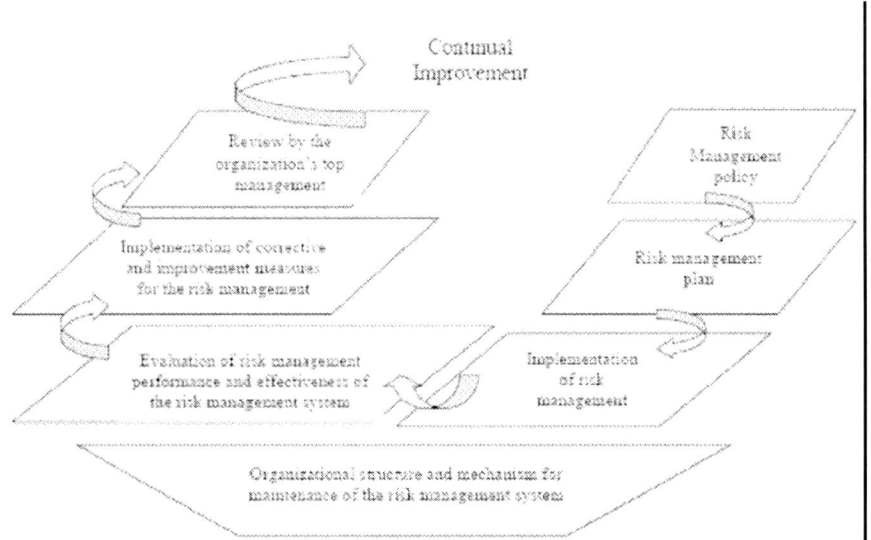

Figure-7. The Japanese Industrial Standard Risk Management System (JSA, 2001).

2.14. Bristish Standard

The British Standard was issued in 2002 as "BSI Technical Committee MS/2 – part 3: Project Management – Guide to the management of business related project risk (Figure-8)." The standard is similar to other risk management frameworks, particularly the Australian New Zealand standard and the UK standard.. It is basically a generic "business" Standard and is fully compatible with the NERAM benchmark standard. The standard shows that the concept of hierarchical decisions in an organization and how this is translated into strategic, tactical, and operational decision making. This is the first framework to show explicitly how risk management can, in a general way, be organized in a complex organization. The standard also presents a restatement of the ALARA (As Low as Reasonably Achievable) principle for positive and negative *consequences* of risks.

There have been a wide variety of frameworks utilized across companies and across countries. Some of these focus narrowly on risk management (rather than enterprise risk management). Others focus on specific industries or specific types of risk. In addition, many of these focus on mechanisms for reducing - rather than managing - risk. By contrast, the COSO *Enterprise Risk Management - Integrated Framework* correctly deals enterprise risk management applicable to all industries and encompassing all types of risk. Moreover, the Framework recognizes that an effective enterprise risk management process must be applied within the context of strategy setting. This is a fundamental difference from most risk models used to date. It starts with the top of the organization and supports an organization's major mission. In addition, many of the pre-existing frameworks stood by themselves, and thus tended to be implemented within functions. As a result, many risk management practices have been implemented in silos (I.e., in one part or one function of the organization). Consequently, risk management may be done very well in one section, but not consider how actions of other parts of the organization affect their risks, or it might not capture the overall significant risks that the organization faces. *The Enterprise Risk Management - Integrated Framework* presents an enterprise-wide perspective of risk and standardizes terms and concepts to promote effective implementation across the organization.

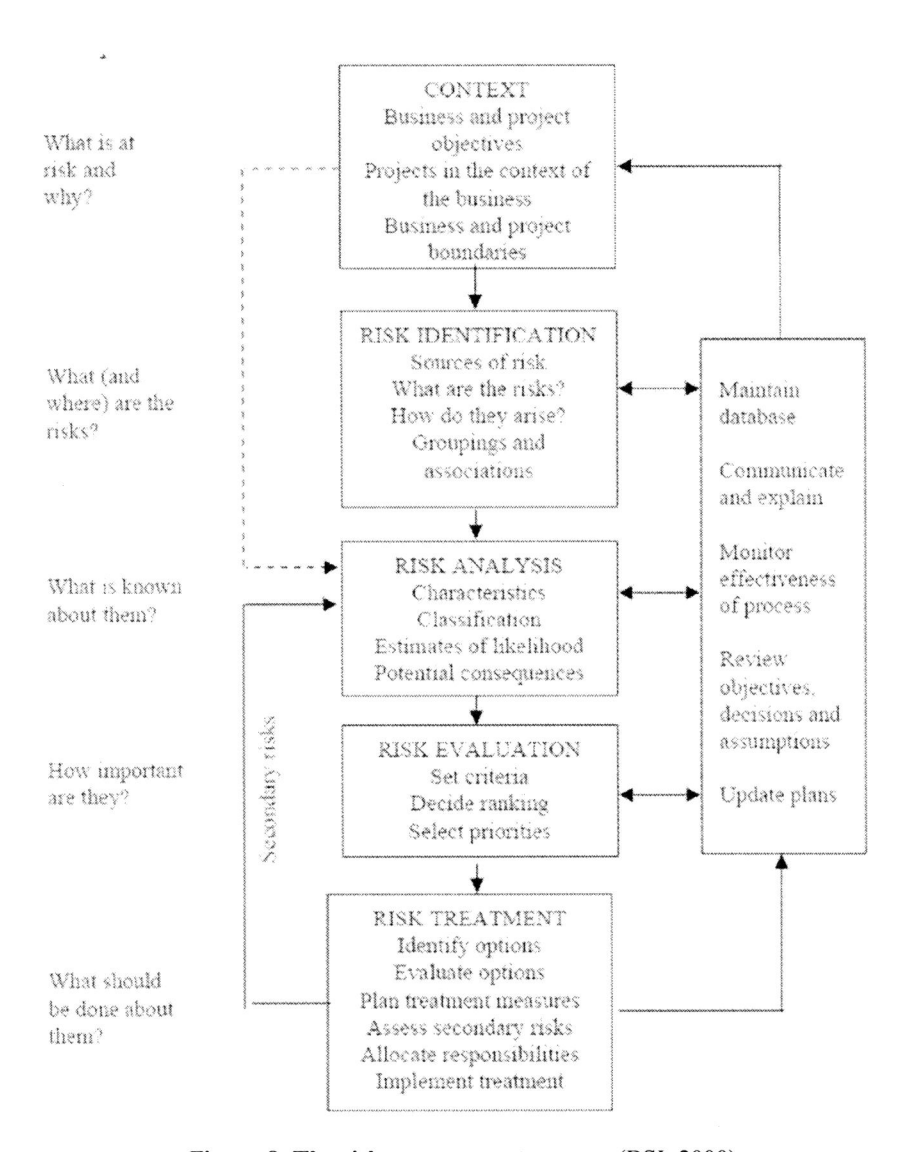

Figure-8. The risk management process (BSI, 2000).

2.15. FAA Safety Risk Management

The System Safety discipline is defined as the application of special technical and managerial skills to the systematic, *forward-looking* identification and control of hazards throughout the life cycle of a project, program, or activity. The primary objective of System Safety is accident prevention. Proactively identifying, assessing, and eliminating or controlling safety-related hazards, to acceptable levels, can achieve accident prevention. A hazard is a condition, event, or circumstance that could lead to or contribute to an unplanned or undesired event. Risk is an expression of the impact of an undesired event in terms of event severity and event likelihood. Throughout this process, hazards are identified, risks analyzed, assessed, prioritized, and results documented for decision-making. The continuous loop process provides for validation of decisions and evaluation for desired results and/or the need for further action.

The System Safety process steps are depicted graphically in the following figure-9. It is a formal and flexible process that generally follows the steps in the FAA's Safety Risk Management Order, 8040.4. A systematic approach to process advance needs proactively searching for opportunities to improve the process at every step, not simply identifying deficiencies after an undesired event. Risk Management has been defined as the process by which Risk Assessment results are integrated with political, social, economic, and engineering considerations for decisions about need/methods for risk reduction.

System Safety Process

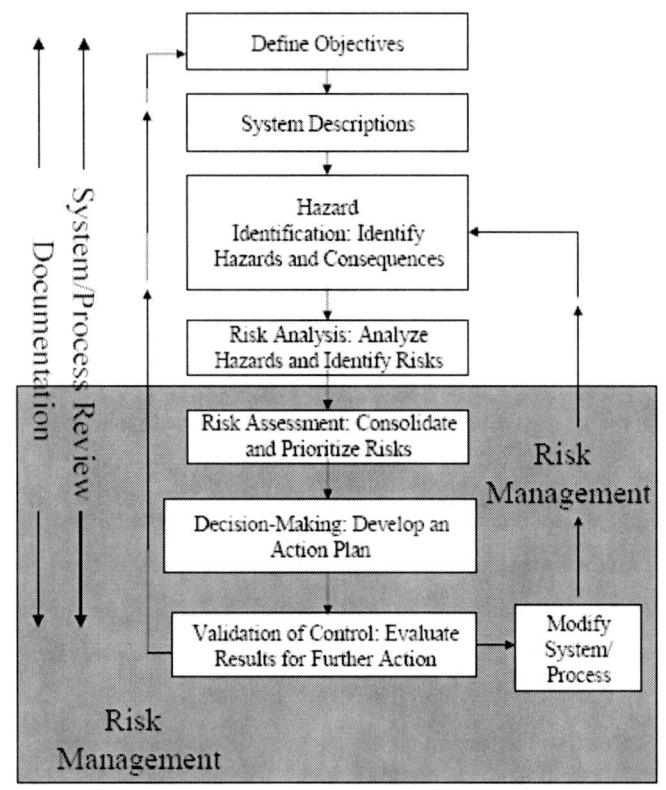

Figure-9. FAA System Safety Process
(http://www.faa.gov/library/manuals/aviation/risk_management/).

3. THE INTEGRATING OF ENTERPRISE RISK MANAGEMENT INTO THE ONGOING MANAGEMENT ACTIVITIES

The business environment is constantly changing and as a consequence implementing ERM is a never ending process. Sustaining ERM requires constant attention by C-level executives, and integration into on-going management initiatives sends a message to associates at all levels of its importance. When ERM is sound business management rather than "the management fad of the month," it becomes an integral part of the DNA of the organizations. Some of the opportunities for integrating ERM in on-going management activities include (IMA, 2006):

• Strategic planning
• Balanced Scorecard (BSC)
• Budgeting
• Business continuity (crisis management)
• Corporate governance and
• Risk disclosures.

The COSO definition of ERM cited previously in paragraph nine states that ERM is part of strategy setting. ERM and strategy setting should be viewed as complimenting each other and not as independent activities. If strategy is formulated without identifying the risks embedded in the strategy and assessing and managing those risks, the strategy is incomplete and at risk of failing. Similarly, if ERM does not begin with identifying risks related to the company's strategy, the effort will be incomplete by failing to identify some of the highest importance risks. Mismanagement of strategic risks has been shown to be the cause for loss of major shareholder value.

In the process of formulating the company's strategy, top management analyzes its strategic alternatives, identifying events that could threaten their achievement. As the risks embedded in each strategic alternative are identified and placed on a risk map the alternative can be evaluated against the organization's capabilities and how it aligns with the risk appetite. Some strategies might be outside the risk appetite of the company and a decision is taking not to pursue them—a decision to avoid the risk. Other strategies may be very risky but can be managed and monitored carefully and thus will be pursued—a decision to accept the risk. Another strategy may be risky but the decision is made to pursue it through a joint venture—a decision to share the risk. Still another alternative strategy with considerable risk embedded in it might be pursued incrementally— a decision to reduce the risk. Strategy formulation is enhanced by ERM because risks are identified, and the strategic alternatives are assessed given the company's risk appetite. In turn, without a good articulated strategy, the foundation for implementing ERM is insufficient. Viewing the two together forms the basis for a strategy-risk-focused organization. ERM ties in closely with corporate governance by:

• improving information flows between the company and the board regarding risks;

• enhancing discussions of strategy and the related risks between executives and the board;

• monitoring key risks by accountants and management with reports to the board;

• identifying acceptable levels of risks to be taken and assumed;

• focusing management on the risks identified;

• improving disclosures to stakeholders about risks taken and risks yet to be managed;

• reassuring the board that management no longer manages risk in silos; and

• knowing which of the organization's objectives are at greatest risk.

ERM is a powerful management tool which is never completed and requires champions at the C-level for its successful implementation. In today's risky world, companies can no longer rely on a silo approach to risk management but need an integrated and holistic perspective of all the risks facing the organisation. A risk-centric organization does not avoid risks but rather knowingly takes risks aligned with its risk appetite (IMA, 2006). Integration of ERM with ongoing management activities serves to embed risk management throughout a company. As company's implement ERM, some best-practices are presented in the following list. ERM is not an option in today's business environment where companies are required to disclose risk factors in the financial reports, and the board of directors regularly questions top management about the company's risk.

List: Hallmarks of Best-Practice ERM

1. Engaged senior management and board of directors that set "the tone from the top" and provide organizational support and resources.

2. Independent ERM function under the leadership of chief risk officer (CRO), who reports directly to the CEO with a dotted line to the board.

3. Top-down governance structure with risk committees at the management and board levels, reinforced by internal and external audit.

4. Established ERM framework that incorporates all of the company's key risks: strategic risk, business risk, operational risk, market risk and credit risk.

5. A risk-aware culture fostered by a common language, training and education, as well as risk-adjusted measures of success and incentives.

6. Written policies with specific risk limits and business boundaries, which collectively represents the risk appetite of the company.

7. An ERM dashboard technology and reporting capability that integrates key quantitative risk metrics and qualitative risk assessments.

8. Robust risk analytics to measure risk concentrations and interdependencies, such as the scenario and simulation models.

9. Integration of ERM in strategic planning, business processes and performance measurement.

10. Optimization of the company's risk-adjusted profitability via risk-based product pricing, capital management and risk-transfer strategies.

Source: James Lam & Associates Inc., *Financial Executive*, January/February 2005:38.

CHAPTER III

ERM BEST PRACTICES

CHAPTER III

BEST PRACTICE CONCEPT IN

THE ENTERPRISE RISK MANAGEMENT

1. BEST PRACTICE DEFINITION

In order to provide comparability and usefulness to the collection of information regarding "best practices" in risk management, it was necessary to first define "best practice" in the context of this project. This definition was developed jointly with KPMG to be used as well in its international study (Performance Management Network Inc, 1999):

> "Not all enterprise risk management practices are best practices, nor would all good practices have relevance or be readily adaptable to the federal public service. It was concluded that a best practice would be a strategy, approach, method, tool or technique that was particularly effective in assisting an organization achieve its objectives for managing risk. A best practice would also be one that was expected to be of value to other organizations."

2. BEST PRACTICE FRAMEWORKS

A best practice framework sets out the areas where best practices would be expected to be of common interest to a variety of organizations. This framework was developed jointly with KPMG to be used as well in its international study. The basic assumption is that an organization invests resources in managing its risks, both strategic and operational, in order to achieve anticipated benefits. These benefits, which are often defined as objectives for managing risk could be any combination of:

- communication for commitment;
- Enhancement of stakeholder value, achievement of corporate objectives;
- Measurement for improved management;
- Support for effective accountability and governance;
- Strengthening of planning and decision processes (synergy, communications, etc.);
- Measurable returns on investments; and,
- Increased confidence of stakeholders.

The best practices framework we have constructed is illustrated as Figure-10.

Dr. Ayse KUCUK YILMAZ

Components	Implementation Strategies	Disciplines & Functions
Practices for integrating management of risk into the managerial framework of an organization	Practices employed to disseminate and integrate management of risk throughout an organization based on a series of "tools".	These are specialized key disciplines and functions where risk management is often integrated and applied at an operational level
• objectives & values communicated • shared responsibility for managing risk and fostering commitment • organization-wide • various strategies • monitored and reported to senior management, governing body and stakeholders	• defined framework • policy • Risk Champion • Task Force • guidelines - training • standard process • defined parameters • software	• Planning • Auditing • Project Management • Finance • Security • Insurance and Asset Management • Environmental Protection • Hazardous Waste Management • Information Technology • Human Resources • Legal • Others

Figure-10. Best Practices Framework Model (Performance Management Network Inc., Review of Canadian Best Practices in Risk Management, April 26, 1999).

Figure-11 provides an overview of the best practices. The "hub," from which all other practices derive, is the organizational philosophy. Taken together, all practices provide the movement to integrate risk management within the organization.

Tools and techniques are the interface with the "road", or the direction and objectives of the organization (KPMG, 1999).

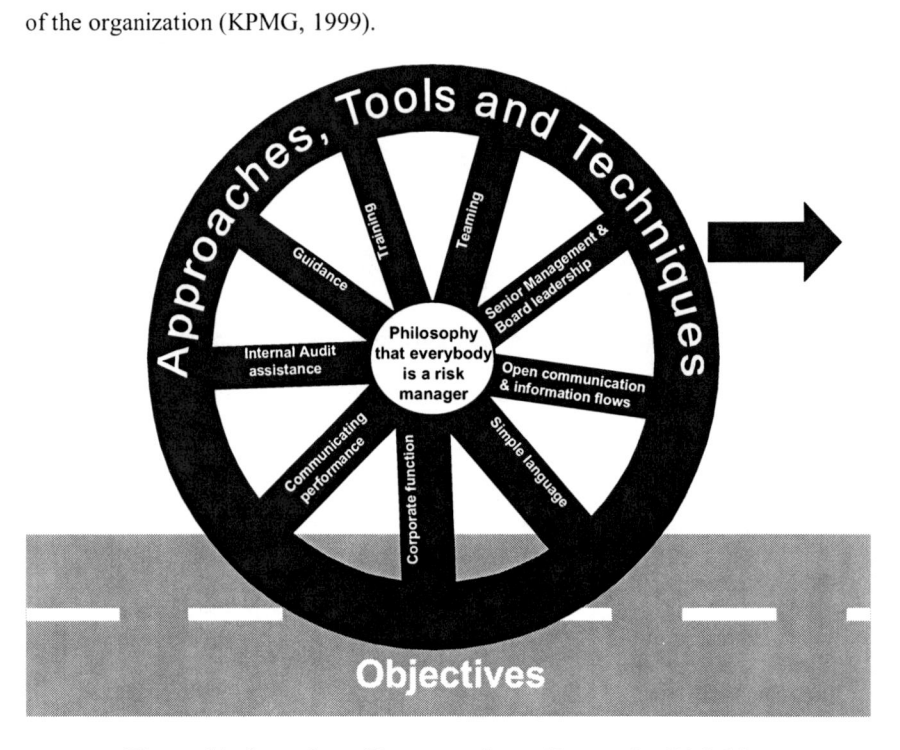

Figure-11. Overview of best practice to Enterprise Risk Management (KPMG, 1999).

Following section explains on the best practices for integrating risk management into management practices.

1. Promoting an organizational philosophy and culture that says everybody is a risk manager.

The predominant practice for integrating risk management is to build an organizational culture in which everybody is a risk manager. Some organizations indicated that this is more important than developing and issuing extensive policies and procedures. Management of risk is embedded in the management philosophy. Employees that take responsibility for their actions and outcomes become risk managers. Ideally, the employees intuitively understand the organization's goals and work towards them. One organization noted that the culture originated in the employee ranks and eventually flowed up to the senior management.

Examples of this practice are:

- Installing restroom mirrors that remind employees that "you are looking at your safety manager".

- Instilling a "sense of excellence" in the culture which encourages people to seek solutions and talk honestly about where they need help.

- Involving all staffs in risk management activities through committees and holding meetings at different work sites.

Sometimes, the culture has to be developed. Practices to achieve this include:

- Setting up the risk management department as a centre of excellence to spread risk management procedures and practices across the organization. The aim is to encourage people to be their own risk managers with the risk management department acting in a support capacity.

- Recruiting on attitude instead of experience, in order to provide outstanding customer service. This helps manage customer risk.

- Introducing penalties. One government introduced a "corporate killing" offense designed to punish corporate directors when they fail to correct unsafe practices that result in death.

- Setting up recognition and reward initiatives that encourage employees to manage risks and take advantage of opportunities.

- Implementing remuneration packages that discourage excessive risk taking. For example, some securities traders have moved to basing traders' remuneration on a formula which compares their profits to those of a benchmark reflecting returns in the marketplace as a whole. In another organization, a "sustainability index" is used to calculate management's bonus. The index is calculated using the cost of electricity, affirmative action achievement and the technical performance of the plant, transmissions and grid.

- Evaluating employees' performance in managing risks, through the performance appraisal process.

- Defining risk management as part of the requirement for all management positions.

- Reinforcing ethics and values by issuing a written code of ethics or communicating them through training, meetings or workshops.

The reported benefit of a risk management culture is that organizations can change more rapidly and can manage risks more effectively.

2. Senior management and/or governing bodies champion risk management and define and communicate acceptable levels of risk

The responsibility for driving risk management is placed highly in the organization. This is also a tool for embedding risk management in the culture. The support of senior management (and/or the governing bodies such as the Board of Directors) is essential. As a start, senior management and the Board must be aware of and understand risk management. There is a wide variety of ways in which the senior leaders are involved in risk management. However, underlying these ways is the role of senior management and the board to send the message internally and externally about the importance of managing risk. Also, it is important that other managers, stakeholders, and employees see their involvement. Managing risk is not just a discussion item for management committees behind closed doors.

Ways that the senior management and Boards lead risk management initiatives include:

- The risk management group uses senior management as sponsors to ensure the risk management message is taken up by their direct reports.

- The Chief Executive Officer attended each meeting for implementing risk management processes. The Chief Financial Officer of the organization was the first senior manager to develop an action plan for an item emerging from a risk workshop.

- Senior Management devotes a day of its annual strategic planning process to identifying and quantifying risks at a strategic level.

- Senior executives sit on an internal control committee and are tasked with providing their department heads with the appropriate internal control mechanisms.

- Board members were asked to think of one risk that kept them awake at night. Then, they were charged with overseeing the management of that risk.

- A safety supervisory board, a subsidiary of the main Board of Directors, reports monthly to the Board of Directors on performance in health, safety and environment.

- Board sign off for new business cases which must include a risk analysis.

- A (external) Council has set the parameters which the risk assessment team uses.

Some organizations report that they set specific responsibilities in risk management for the Board and senior management. The Board may provide skilled guidance such as identifying the principal risks to the business, ensuring that appropriate systems are implemented to manage the risks, ensuring the integrity of the control and management systems, and defining responsibilities and monitoring major risks. Management is accountable for coordinating the risk management and identifying, evaluating, controlling and reporting risks. Most importantly, the Board of Directors or senior management, defines, develops and approves a Risk Policy.

The key message of the Risk Policy is the level of risk that the key process is willing to accept. The policy might also state roles and responsibilities and practices for managing risk. Managers require clear direction on risk tolerance. That direction must come from the governing body or senior management. Workshops are another way to communicate the tolerances.

3. Establishing open communication channels

The practices reported to demonstrate that open communication is necessary for risk management to succeed. For example, teams rely on communication to address risks and achieve objectives. Also, many report that open communication is a way to easily integrate risk management into existing processes. If communication is not there, risk management cannot be "everybody's business". Managers require direct communication channels up, down and across their business units to help identify risks and take appropriate actions. New looser-information based structures are replacing traditional organization structures with defined reporting relationships. Information must be shared.

Examples of open and good communication are:

- Using the intranet to communicate the organization's efforts and involve all employees in managing risk. It is also used to communicate objectives.

- Appointing managers whose only task is to communicate risks to employees.

- Holding quarterly meetings of a risk management committee to review and discuss the organization's exposure and protection measures.

- Using the risk management function to communicate objectives.

- Promoting awareness of risk management issues through monthly, quarterly and annual reports. The reports focus on areas that require help from the risk management group.

- Making presentations to senior management and/or the governing body on the risk management process.

- Encouraging people to discuss mistakes.

4. Using teams and committees

Informal and formal teams are a mechanism that many organizations report they are using to manage risks. Teams were cited in a number of situations such as the management of financial risk, construction projects, workers' compensation, health and safety, insurance, contract management, transport, treasury management, project management, new product development. Teaming brings to light the dynamics between disciplines, brings together various risk attitudes, and brings fresh thinking to issues, opportunities, strategies and solutions. It is perceived as a way to focus diverse disciplines on common objectives, one of which is minimizing risk. Teams provide balance. Also, teams pollinate a concern for risk management throughout the organization, rather than being the concern of a function or discipline. While the practice of teaming is recognized as a "best practice", there was no common practice concerning the composition of the team.

The composition of formal risk management teams included:

- Line management, treasury, audit, compliance, public relations, human resources and risk management professionals.
- Specific risk management teams for each of contract management control, health and safety, insurance, transport and treasury management.
- Multi-disciplinary teams for projects and product development.
- Seeding management teams with individuals with varying risk attitudes.
- A cross-functional risk management committee with representation from operating units and treasury/finance, human resources and risk management.
- A risk management strategy steering group where all major functions are represented.
- A risk management committee composed of division heads.

In other cases, various disciplines are encouraged to work together, such as:

- The audit group, the Chief Financial Officer, senior management, and treasury.

- Workers' compensation claims department, medical department, corporate ethics department, security, human resources and legal department jointly taking on risk management responsibilities.

- A claims coordinator working closely with the human resources department.

- A team of loss control specialists and claim handlers available during construction projects.

- A project team of corporate audit, finance and control, and a chartered accountant which supports managers' self-assessment of risk.

Teams provide a wider perspective and look at various angles of risks and consequences. To operate, teams require open communication.

5. Using a simple, common business risk language

In order to integrate risk management into other management processes, the terminology should be easily understandable by managers. The approaches should also be simple to understand and use. By developing a common business risk language, managers can discuss with individuals from the boardroom to the boiler room in terms that everybody understands. This is important also in cases where everybody is expected to manage risks. The risk management approaches and processes must be simple to be accepted by business management. Organizations have reported that complex, intellectual tools have proven to be unsuccessful. Others caution that the approaches must also be flexible to be meaningful across business units. Though the process must be simple and useful across units, the process should not be oversimplified. The designers of the process must balance simplicity with usefulness.

6. Setting up a corporate risk management function

Many organizations have set up a responsibility centre for risk management. Some units are headed by a Chief Risk Officer (CRO) who defines consistent approaches to managing risk. As the organizational risk champion, the CRO is responsible for providing leadership and establishing and maintaining risk awareness across the organization. The CRO might also set up risk control objectives, a risk framework, and design ways to measure risk. These senior risk managers must have strong persuasion skills. The risk manager must deal with business risks, not just insurable risks. In this way, their importance within the organization increases.

7. Communicating risk management performance

A handful of organizations reports to management and stakeholders/shareholders on risks and risk management performance ways of reporting are:

- The Internal Control department presents two reports annually to the President. The reports communicate the results of monitoring risk. Each Operating Division is required to prepare an annual report on its monitoring results for the Internal Control Department.

- Business Unit Managers are basically needed to report three times annually to the Finance and Risk subcommittee of the Board. The reports outline the units' top ten risks and how they are managed.

- Managers advise the Board on the risks of their ventures and key shareholders/stakeholders have their say.

8. Internal Audit and/or the Audit Committee assists in implementing risk management

The internal audit function plays a key role in implementing ERM throughout an organization. Examples of this practice are:

- Facilitating self-assessment workshops.
- Monitoring and reporting on the management of significant risks.
- Providing advice.
- Raising awareness of risk management among managers.
- Identifying critical risks and preparing "watching briefs" on them.
- Monitoring compliance in key areas, such as legislative requirements.
- Reviewing processes for managing risks.
- Communicating objectives for managing risk.
- Sitting on the risk management committee.

9. Guidance

Providing guidance is an important practice for integrating risk management. Guidance is provided indirectly (documents) or directly (advice). Examples of this practice are:

- A guidance paper for government departments that are preparing public sector construction projects. "Essential Requirements for Construction Procurement" integrates value and risk management with project management.
- A tool kit for agencies of the government. The kit enables agencies to self-assess their position relative to current best practices. It also helps them move to the best practice using generic improvement strategies.
- Internal consulting services provided by the risk management unit.
- A forum of managers. Managers are able to identify their problems/risks. The forum allows the sharing of best practices. Action items are proposed to deal with the risk. Another advantage is all line managers are now aware of the risk and the action items.

- A legislative agency that makes recommendations to agency management for reducing risk. The recommendations have been proven successful in other agencies.

10. Enterprise Risk Management Training

ERM training, as part of a corporate training curriculum, gradually assists integrate risk. Topic areas include: risk assessments; best practices; legislative requirements; safety; objectives for managing risk; risk-awareness training to ensure that all managers consider risk. Applicability criteria are given following;

Applicability Criteria to Best Enterprise Risk Management Practice

During KPMG'S analysis, they determined that some of the criteria related very well to the best practices. When organizations would explain their best practice it became evident they were applying many of original criteria. However, some of these criteria did not relate well to any of the best practices. These criteria appear to relate to "risk management" but not to a best practice for risk management. KPMG's original criteria were as follows:

- Has broad applicability, beyond the protection of assets and people
- Fosters a supportive work environment
- Supports innovation
- Improves service delivery ,, e.g., efficiency, effectiveness
- Improves access to government / government services
- Facilitates management decision-making
- Promotes sound resource allocation
- Is easily understood and used (plain language, user-friendliness)
- Helps managers understand the context and implications of risk.

- Demonstrates communication / involvement with stakeholders
- Facilitates cultural shifts and change management
- Builds on existing knowledge, lessons learned in the organization.
- Considers opportunity costs
- Has a clear and potentially applicable accountability or governance framework
- Makes effective use of an audit and evaluation resources
- Links horizontally in the organization
- Integrates well with the existing management framework, processes and practices

List-2: Enterprise Risk Management Best Practices Reference Chart (KMPG).

Best Practices
1. Commitment from the top
2. Face-to-face workshops for developing senior management
3. Targeting "natural fit" areas
4. Risk/Control Self-Assessment sessions
5. "Learning by doing" method of training and support
6. Planning / reporting on risks
7. Developing a core competency first
8. Messaging about foundations and monitoring
9. Risk Management Policy Framework
10. Experienced, committed senior managers to lead initiative
11. Risk perception and risk communication
12. Risk framework
13. Regular attention to the risk management process

14. Risk management committee
15. Utilizing the best of existing structure to work with
16. Independent office
17. Comprehensive Risk Management Handbook
18. Customized training program
19. Clearly defining "risk"
20. Scenario planning
21. Planning with Partners

3. KEY CONCLUSIONS

The following key conclusions concerning ERM from analysis of best practices by KMPG:

• **Enterprise Risk management, like comptrollership, is a mind-set:** Managers should be conscious of risk management and integrate it into their other management practices. Overly bureaucratic and complex processes will submerge ERM into irrelevance. Managers need the flexibility to use techniques that make sense for them and their operation. However, the technique must allow for the roll up and comparison of operating unit results at the corporate level. Specialists need to be available to assist managers.

• **Enterprise Risk Management and corporate ethics functions should work together:** The information we gathered indicates that ERM and ethics programs are related. For example, a written code of ethics is a mechanism to communicate the values of the organization and the related risks. An ethics program for government employees is viewed as a way to sensitize employees to ethical issues or risks affecting the key entity's values.

• **Enterprise Risk Management is a dynamic process:** As the business needs and business risks change, new processes or tools for managing the risks are required. How organizations are performing at managing risk must also be monitored and continuously improved. Risk assessments are not a "one-off" exercise.

- **Many functional specialists will play a role in Enterprise Risk Management:** The review of best practices indicates that many functional specialists will play a role in managing risk. These include specialists in information technology, human resources, communications and financial management.

- **Enterprise Risk Management must be adequately resourced:** Senior management must be committed to supporting the initiative with the required resources. Investments will be required in training, developing processes and techniques, management systems and setting up specialist groups.

Factors such as the global pace of change, resource restraint, growing openness, transparency and accountability and significant continual organizational change present a demanding case for better management of risk. It is a difficult exercise to attempt to determine tangible benefits that measure the distance from a course followed to a course not followed. However, it was evident from each of the public and private sector organizations contacted that they are convinced that their investments of time, money and staff resources in more systematic *management of risk* have been beneficial to achieving their respective corporate objectives. Not one of our respondents expressed regrets at having embarked upon this course of action. These organizations are continuing to see both medium and longer term benefits and causal results which are sufficient to satisfy them and their key stakeholders of the value of the investments they have already made and are continuing to make.

For the companies to successfully implement a more comprehensive approach to management of risk the best practices and lessons gleaned from other public and private sector organizations will prove to be instructive and will reduce the need to "re-invent the wheel". However, it must be acknowledged that each federal agency will nonetheless need to customize and adapt these best practices and lessons to suit its own particular culture and environment.

Leadership and support must be visibly and regularly demonstrated from the top. It was also explicitly recognized by most of the organizations examined that moving toward more systematic management of risk required a change in their organizational culture. More particularly they needed to develop and promote an environment of support for innovation and more conscious risk-taking , with the corollary recognition that there would be "misses" as well as "hits". It is also clear that management of risk cannot take hold and be practiced routinely by management and staff in an organization without dedicated up-front and ongoing investments. A framework laying out the strategic elements and specifying the implementation parameters for the particular organization is an essential initial product. Implementation strategies may vary, dependent upon the objectives, but should contain some investments in training, communication, promotion and process support to ensure that there is common understanding, management and communications. Finally there should be a designated responsibility centre to serve as both the source of "expert" support to others within the organization, and to sustain the process and ongoing communications of both successes and lessons learned.

CHAPTER IV
THE BEST ERM PRACTICES IN THE AIRTRANSPORTATION SECTOR: AIRLINE & AIRPORT BUSINESS

CHAPTER IV

THE BEST ENTERPRISE RISK MANAGEMENT PRACTICES IN AIRTRANSPORTATION SECTOR: AIRLINE AND AIRPORT BUSINESS

1. INTRODUCTION

Air transport is one of the fastest growing industries of the world, evidenced by the demand for air travel that increased three-fold between 1980 and 2000, and which is set to double by 2020. This illustrates how essential the industry is to modern life; few people could imagine or would want a world without air travel – since the benefits of being linked to all regions worldwide via a network of air routes are increasingly significant in terms of access, time savings, economic benefits and safety. From an economic point of view, air transport is essential for world business and tourism. It creates jobs and facilitates the expansion of world trade by opening up new market opportunities. It also attracts businesses to locations in the developed and developing world thereby satisfying the mobility requirements of a growing portion of the world's population – and moves products and services quickly over long distances enabling economic and social participation by outlying communities. From a social perspective, air transport forms a unique global transport network linking people, countries and cultures safely and efficiently. It is increasingly accessible to a greater number of people who can now afford to travel by air for leisure and business purposes. In environmental terms, air transport has been able to reduce or contain its environmental impact by continually improving its fuel consumption, reducing noise and introducing new, more sustainable technologies (Rochat, 2007).

Airline and airport business should have ERM for achieving to sustainability objectives. As it can be observed the following figure-12, ERM implementation is an essential element of the best sustainability management in the airport business.

ERM is the most important support to balancing approach to assessing products, services and business activities using the following criteria as indicators to essence of sustainability (Rochat, 2007):

1- Financial Criteria

- Economically sustainable
- Technologically feasible
- Operationally viable

2- Environmental Criteria

- Environmentally robust
- Generational sensitive
- Capable of Continuous learning

3- Social Criteria

- Socially desirable
- Culturally acceptable.

Dr. Ayse KUCUK YILMAZ

Figure-12. Enterprise Risk Mangement to Sustainable Airport Business (James M. Crites, Redefining Sustainability for the Aviation Industry, Stanford Court Hotel, San Francisco, March 4, 2007).

The airline and airport business and related industry have been through more structural changes in the past decade than most. The airline and airports face a number of risks in today's climate. Airlines are operating in a very competitive environment. Airline and airports are exposed to the risk of catastrophic loss. Airlines and airports are operating to the highest standards of safety and security and are work closely with all the relevant authorities to ensure that customer safety is paramount always. The airline and airports are characterized by low profit margins and high fixed costs. The air transport business is sensitive to both cyclical and seasonal changes. Competition in the sector is intense and the decline in average ticket prices has been considerable as a result of over capacity and the changed market situation.

The airline industry tends to experience adverse financial results during general economic downturns and recent airline financial results may lead to significant changes in air transportation industry. The 2001 terrorist attacks seriously harmed airline industry and the increased risk of additional attacks or military involvement in Iraq, the Middle East or other regions may harm the industry in the future. Increases in fuel costs would harm business to airlines. Airlines are often affected by factors beyond their control, including weather conditions, traffic congestion at airports and increased security measures, any of which could harm airline's operating results and financial condition. Changes in government regulations imposing additional requirements and restrictions on airline operations could increase their operating costs and result from in service delays and disruptions. The airline industry is characterized by low profit margins and high fixed costs, and many airlines may be unable to compete effectively against other airlines with greater financial resources or lower operating costs. Insurance costs have increased substantially as a consequence of the September 11th terrorist attacks, and further increases in insurance costs would harm to business. Also, Substantial consolidation in the airline industry could harm their business to many airlines. Their reputation and financial results could be harmed in the event of an accident or incident involving their aircraft (Jetblue, 2004).

ERM is launched at Delta following the terrorist attacks of September 11, 2001. The Delta ERM team worked to map key risks affecting these core categories of business operations (Delta airline, 2005): Financial, Operational, Compliance, Legal, Security, Human Capital, Technology, Political and Reputation. Duncan (Delta CRO) noted that "ERM is ultimately about changing culture and behavior and driving decision making and measurable results." He also said that "ERM is a matter of future survivability" and that getting ERM underway is more important than trying to develop the most sophisticated risk management system at the start. In essence – "just start" (Delta airline, 2005).

Since the mid-1980s, the world airline industry has got a period of significant structural, institutional and regulatory changes. The increased competition and recent recession have led to be severe and widespread losses in the international airline industry, and forced carriers to undertake major restructuring in order to improve efficiency and reduce costs (Oum and Yu, 1998).

Airline earnings are highly volatile. It is commonly believed that one of the most important sources of volatility in airline earnings are fuel prices. Actually, airlines exposure to this risk is believed to be greater than their exposures to either interest rate or foreign exchange risk (Quinn, 1996).

2. THE AIRLINE RISK MANAGEMENT SURVEY

Aon and Airline Business magazine have completed the second Airline Risk Management Survey. The anonymous survey is carried out at the end of 2006, with over 60% of the top 200 airlines globally by revenue offering views on the evolution of risk management during the year. Around two thirds of respondents described themselves as major or flag airlines, in comparison to just less than half in 2006. This suggests that the survey is gaining traction as the industry's major players recognize the value of an independent, anonymous survey of their risk tolerance. Respondents are again well spread geographically. Just under a third of came from Europe, and just under a quarter were from both Asia Pacific and North America. Reflecting the larger organisations that responded, the proportion of operations claiming to have company-wide risk management strategies rose from 67% in 2005/6 to 86% in 2006/7.

The average risk strategy length is 2.5 years compared to the 3.3 years reported last year. This reflects the rapid evolution of the industry and the recognition of the need for flexibility to take advantage of opportunities as changes occur. Equally, the number of organisations with risk strategies of longer than four years has dropped to 14% from 39% in 2005/6, and nearly three quarters of operations have interim strategies. Reflecting the soft airline insurance market, risk management budgets fell to 1.6% percent of total revenue, from 2.1% in 2005/6.

There is also less pessimism about market direction in comparison with the last survey. In 2005/6, 44% of respondents expected risk management costs to increase during 2006, but in 2006/7 this has fallen to 31%. Similarly, only 21% of respondents expected risk management costs to decline for their 2006/7 renewal, a number that has risen to 35% for the 2007/8 renewal. That said, this may reflect the larger number of flag carriers and majors that participated in the survey this year, given that airline insurance market's propensity to reward scale. Interestingly, the proportion of total risk spending represented by insurance coverage has fallen from around 70% to just over 60% in 2006/7. Nearly 40% of this is comprised of mandatory coverage.

Attitude to risk is broadly unchanged, with 74% of respondents comfortable to retain some level in the 2006/7 survey in comparison to 68% last year. The number of operations that said they were comfortable retaining a high level of risk has fallen from 8% to 4% between the two surveys, again potentially a function of the respondent profile.

Reflecting the level of debate in certain regions and the current focus on corporate responsibility, environmental pollution has become the highest future risk requirement, having been sixth in the 2005/6 survey. This change knocked computer crime insurance into second place, while business interruption climbed to become the third highest additional risk that organisations will be looking to insure against in the next three years. Risk priorities have only changed slightly, with the aircraft accident, aircraft-related war/terrorism and property (damage) still the three highest priorities. Premium price remains the main issue for most of respondents, while transparency, gratifyingly, has fallen in importance below financial strength and claims services. "The results prove the value of carrying out this in-depth survey," says Steve Doyle, Aon Global Specialist Industries. "It ensures that we as risk management consultants and insurance brokers can match our offerings to the needs of the airline industry, and make sure that we provide a full range of risk services that meet our clients' evolving requirements. It also lets organisations benchmark their approach to risk management and insurance against their competitors."

Airlines are spending at least $8.36 billion a year on risk management, with around 70% – or $5.86 billion – going on insurance premiums, according to new research into airline risk management trends. Insurance premiums fell significantly in 2005, but despite the expectation within the risk management community that this downward trend will continue in 2006, albeit less markedly, there is considerable anxiety about the cost of premiums. Some 60% of respondents highlight it as one of the most important insurance industry issues affecting the aviation business. Risk experts are linking this concern to the fragility of airline finances, plus newly perceived business and terrorism risks.

The first detailed snapshot of airline risk management issues, commissioned by *Airline Business* in association with insurance broking firm Aon, reveals that the legacy of the terror attacks in the USA on 11 September 2001 continues to have a significant impact on risk management. Aviation premiums are on average 15.5% higher than pre-9/11 levels and war terrorism insurance and restrictions on cover are the major risk issues facing the airlines, according to nearly a third of risk managers surveyed in the study.

In this climate, it is unsurprising that nearly half of the airlines surveyed are expecting to increase their overall risk management spend in 2006 and many are already planning to widen the range of insurances that they buy in the future, with computer crime topping the list of additional policy requirements.

The Airline Risk Management Survey 2005 was launched last autumn with the aim of reaching a better understanding of the matters and trends within airline risk management and to establish some industry benchmarks against which airlines can measure and monitor their own performance. For research breaking new ground among the airlines, the response rate was positive – 51 airlines took part, accounting for 41% of the world's top 200 airlines by total revenue.

Risk strategies

The survey shows that risk management has a high profile within airline businesses: not only do two-thirds of airlines have a company-wide risk management strategy, which, on average looks just over three years into the future, overall responsibility for risk is taken at the boardroom level in 75% of airlines, with the chief executive's office making the decision whether to avoid, retain or transfer risk in 45% of airlines.

Risk management, on average, accounts for 2.1% of airlines' total revenue – apply that to the revenues of the world's top 200 airlines, and you are talking about a budget of at least $8.36 billion per annum, with an average of 70.1% channeled into insurance. But, as Aon's global practice manager for aviation and aerospace Steven Doyle points out, 2% is a small amount of the industry's overall costs when fuel and staffing each account for about 25%. "Seventy percent of risk management spends is insurance, which highlights the fact that insurance is cheap and a good way of transferring risk," he says.

The survey shows that premium rates overall dropped significantly for most of airlines in 2005, with the greatest decreases on the aviation side and respondents are for the most part forecasting that rates in 2006 will remain unchanged or reduce slightly, with the greatest reductions again on the aviation side. The overall aviation (hull, liability, war and excess) premium unit cost for 2004-5 averages out at $157,000 per aircraft and $1.68 per passenger, reinforcing Doyle's view that insurance is value for money. "There were about 1.6 billion passengers in 2001 and the market generated $4 billion in premiums, so it's gone from about $2.50 per passenger to $1.68," he says. Aviation premiums are, on average, 15.5% higher than before 9/11, but although the industry's loss record has been good in the last four years, traffic and passenger number have risen significantly, increasing the exposure to risk. "We estimate exposure has grown in the region of 30-40% since 9/11, so if the premium is only up 15% [airlines] are better off than they were, even if they are paying more dollars," says Doyle.

Around the globe airline risk managers are surprised by this average hike. Eva Dahlberg, director of SAS Group insurance, and Toshio Akama, board member of Japan Airlines Capital, the financial services subsidiary of JAL, both say the figure is lower than they expected. "After 9/11 aviation insurance premiums jumped up. Gradually, the premiums have come down, but in consequence of the attitude of capital providers to the aviation insurance market, it is unlikely that premiums will return to the same levels that existed before 9/11," says Akama.

At Iberia, chief financial officer Enrique Dupuy suggests that in Europe the level of premiums are substantially higher than the 15.5% research average, as premiums for excess third-party war risk liability (AVN 52), which did not exist pre-9/11, were not included. However, in the USA, Pete Fahrenthold, managing director–risk management at Continental Airlines, is not surprised by the level, observing that before 9/11 premiums were too low to maintain a stable market for the cover.

"The key trends impacting on the aviation market now versus pre-9/11 are the increase in exposure arising from the Airbus A380 [500-600 passenger loads and higher hull values/composite construction]; the higher returns available for capital placed to support other lines of aviation cover for airlines (e.g.propertyinsuranceorgener al aviationinsurance and); In addition, the impact of 11 on 9 / 11 on the underwriter's perception of where terrorism risks exist for a given airline-ie, they exist everywhere now Airline ," he says. Airline anxiety about the cost of premiums – 80 % of respondents cited it among the insurance industry placed concerns affecting airlines and 60 % placed it among there On the one hand, many insurance policies are mandatory ones that airlines hope not to claim against. "They are buying a commodity they never wish to use, so it will always be viewed as expensive," observes Aon's Steven Doyle. However, pressure to cut costs and the embattled financial position of many of the world's airlines are also a factor colouring attitudes. "The environment for airlines is quite tough. We are all fighting bad financials and even if they recover, it is still a little fragile," says Dahlberg. "The premium cost is substantial these days, some insurance are mandatory, and if you have fragile finances, it is important that you can insure against risks." Financially hard-pressed carriers generate a climate of concern among their staff, shareholders and their insurers, which makes it harder to keep the lid on costs. "Approximately 50% of US airline capacity has been/is in bankruptcy. This creates trepidation and uncertainty on the part of insurers for executive liability lines such as directors' and officers' liability and fiduciary liability because shareholders and/or employees become dissatisfied and may file the suit," says a US airline source, pointing out that insurers typically react to this situation with a combination of charging more, cutting back on capacity and/or withdrawing from providing the coverage as a whole.

"Workers compensation claims for employees injuries sustained on the job typically increase for companies in financial duress as employees become more concerned about layoffs and the personal financial outlay to meet medical plan deductibles increase," adds the US airline source. "Also the internal functions associated with the management of these types of claims become outsourced and the level of scrutiny for cost containment may not [be] at the same level when company staff is monitoring the claims."

Terrorism and new business risks are also fuelling the airline concern about premiums. Iberia's Dupuy says the threat of dirty bombs, plus the lack of stable, competitive capacity for war and terrorism risks, will have an impact on future insurance costs. "Additionally new perceived risks – directors' and officers' responsibilities, credit risks, overbooking and operating risks, loss of uses, credit card acquirers risk etc – will increase the factors of the insurance bill and make it difficult to come back to the glory days of pre-9/11." mind, it is not surprising that 24% of risk managers in the study cite war and terrorism in general as the major risk facing the aviation industry and a further 30% believe it is specifically war terrorism insurance and restrictions on cover. The majority – 55% – believe that government insurance/limitation of liability is the most realistic way forward. The backdrop to this issue is moves within the commercial insurance market to reduce cover for weapons of mass destruction through policy endorsements and the fact that airlines around the globe are not competing on a level playing field: the US government keeps to provide its own carriers with third-party war risk cover while most of the other governments in the world are not willing to bear this risk. The varying levels of optimism among risk specialists about the likelihood of achieving the airlines' preferred resolution seems to reflect their geographical perspective.

"European governments have not intervened; they have even become stricter in the legal insurance requirements after 9/11. I do not think they will in the short term take a limitation of liability for airlines," says Dupuy. "Although they accept that terrorism has and could use our industry [our aircraft] to target governments, they do not want to act as insurers, even insurers of last resort. Their view is that they will act reactively, when there is an insurance market failure as a consequence of a major accident and possibly when the airlines are about to stop flying." At Continental, Fahrenthold is a firm advocate of governments around the world providing coverage or at the very least, a backstop to the insurance market's terrorism cover. "A liability cap is also necessary if the commercial insurers are to be expected to provide any useable level of coverage. I believe that various governments would be willing to provide a cap under the right circumstances," he says. "Discussions have been ongoing between IATA, ATA [US Air Transport Association] and ICAO on possible structures that would be a blend of commercial insurance, governmental guarantees and a liability cap, and an ICAO proposal is being drafted."

Although overall risk management costs declined in 2005 – the research shows they decreased for 48% and stayed with the same for 26% this year – 44% of airlines are forecasting their spend will increase in 2006 and 35% expect costs to stay with the same. JAL suggests security issues and avian flu may be driving up risk spend. Dahlberg at SAS suggests some of the increased spend may be going on education to ensure teams are up to date and on information systems – echoed by Dupuy at Iberia, who says the new international accounting standards and corporate governance risk guidelines imply new investments in software and consulting.

Another factor may be high jet fuel costs resulting in more airlines having to develop fuel hedging program or hedging more intensively. "I suppose that the growth of airline travel [low cost] and the setting of new airlines in emerging economies [India, China, Latin America] might be increasing the need for risk management solutions associated with higher levels of hedging," says Dupuy.

According to the research, the top five insurance risk priorities are the aircraft accident, aircraft-related war/ terrorism, property damage, general liability and directors' and officers' liabilities. This is not very surprising considering that insurance covering most of these risks is mandatory for many airlines. However, looking beyond operational essentials, airlines are earmarking extra risks to insure against in the future, with 37% planning to insure against computer crime, 30% against credit risks and 22% against loss of reputation. "The increase in web-based ticketing and the greater use of check-in kiosks at airports and online check-in has increased our demand for 'network risk'insurance. The insurance market for these products has been evolving and improving, and I believe that we will purchase some form of this cover in the near future," says Fahrenthold.

Changes in the structure of the travel agent network and the growth of online sales has also increased awareness of credit risks, threats to liquidity and cash flow and Dupuy points out a number of airlines are now managing agency credit risk.

Although loss of reputation is at the bottom of current airline insurance policies, branding is an increasingly big issue for airlines and fears about loss of the brand and reputation can be tied in to the emergence of highly branded low-cost carriers and frequent flyer branding for the big alliances. Aon's Steven Doyle points to the example of Virgin Atlantic Airways which delayed delivery of its A380s because Los Angeles International airport was not going to be ready. "They did not want to compromise with passenger experience, so brand is of the highest importance," explains Doyle.

There is also increasing awareness of the "fragility of reputation in our sector and the big negative impact that can be derived from a reputation problem," according to Dupuy. "In my view our industry is looking with much more care and attention to these new reputations and image risks." This emerging risk will be one of the ones to watch in next year's Airline Risk Management Survey as the research starts to tease out the forthcoming trends and the study establishes itself as the leading benchmark for risk management.

Exhibit 2 Airline Risk Factors

Generally, airline risks are grouped in the four main categories (figure-13). They are;

Strategic risks are defined by business design choices and how these interact with external factors. A challenge from a new form of competition shifts in customer preference and industry consolidation are all examples. Many of these challenges may be mitigated through traditional responses, such as a change in corporate culture. Nevertheless, other risks can be lessened from the outset through the basic design of the business. For example, Southwest Airlines has a model that attracts customers in good times and in bad because it is simple, and cost and operationally effective. It is also not under the influence of the reliability problems that bedevil network carriers.

Other design choices further lower the carrier's risk exposure. For example, use of secondary airports insulates it from direct competitive pressure and speeds aircraft turns. Low debt levels make the company less vulnerable to interest rate fluctuations. Furthermore, profit sharing and a fun culture reduce labour difficulties (O'Toole, 2002).

Financial risks involve the management of capital and cash, including external factors that affect the variability and predictability of revenue and cash flow - such as general economic conditions or currency exchange rates. Beyond hazard risks, techniques to mitigate financial risks are the most advanced, primarily because there is a large third-party market dedicated to the effort, including banks, credit specialists, derivative markets and others. Financial solutions may include the design and placement of financial transactions, for example, structured finance, derivatives, insurance, contingent financing and debt/equity offerings. Other, new approaches could push supposing even further in this area (O'Toole, 2002).

Operational risks arise from the tactical aspects of running the process, such as crew scheduling, accounting and information systems and e-commerce activities. Many airlines have processes in place to mitigate the most obvious operational risks, such as business interruption, but fail to address more subtle issues, for example working with government to shape regulatory issues which cost millions in operational inefficiencies and legal actions (O'Toole, 2002).

Operations can also be reshaped to reduce risk through familiar concepts such as process re-engineering, contingency planning or improved communications. The challenge is to look at risks holistically, as well as evaluating each potential response through the lens of impact on shareholder value. Then strategies can be clearly set to mitigate risk wherever it resides (O'Toole, 2002).

3. BEST PRACTICE SAMPLES TO ENTERPRISE RISK MANAGEMENT IN AIRLINE BUSINESS

In this section, the selected best samples of airline enterprise risk management practice are presented:

- LUFTHANSA
- CONTINENTAL AIRLINES
- DELTA AIRLINES
- FINNAIR
- AUSTRIAN AIRLINE
- SILVERJET
- JETBLUE

3.1. Lufthansa Risk Management

As an international airline Lufthansa is exposed both to general entrepreneurial risks and to industry-specific risks. Key areas of exposure are capacity and utilisation risks, strategy-related risks, political risks, operational risks, procurement risks, labour agreement risks, IT risks plus financial and treasury management risks. Steering with circumspection between opportunities and business risks is integral to corporate management. Consequently, the Group's risk early warning and management system consists of a multiplicity of components that are systematically embedded in its entire organisational and operational structure respectively, of its subsidiaries. Risk management is regarded as a prime responsibility of the managers of all business entities and of the process and project managers in the Group companies.

A Risk Management Committee makes sure that risks are identified and assessed continuously across functions and processes. The Committee is responsible for verifying the system's effectiveness and its ongoing refinement. It reports regularly to the Executive Board, further develops the basic principles of risk policy and oversees their compliance. It also communicates the Group's risk policy, defines the documentation requirements and initiates any necessary reviews of specific aspects of the risk management system by the internal auditing department.

All significant risks potentially affecting the Group's results or threatening its existence are documented in a structured "risk map"; this is regularly updated and augmented. Significant risks are defined as dangers which per se might make damage equal to at least one third of the result necessary to maintain the Company's inherent value. Due account is taken of potential interdependencies between different risks.

The measures, specified by the ERM system to ensure the timely identification, limitation and elimination of those risks, are themselves regularly reviewed and reinforced. Above and beyond appropriate insurance solutions, countermeasures are in place to resolve individual risk situations.

An analysis of risks, together with possibilities of limiting and overcoming them, also forms an integral part of the Company's strategy development process and is incorporated into Operational Group Planning. Lufthansa reduces risk of rising costs as a consequence of changes in fuel prices, interest rates and exchange rates through a systematic financial management strategy.

Lufthansa is exposed both to general entrepreneurial risks and to industry-specific risks. Key areas of exposure are capacity and utilisation risks, strategy-related risks, political risks, operational risks, procurement risks, labour agreement risks, IT risks plus financial and treasury management risks.

The ERM strategy of Deutsche Lufthansa AG allows the Company to exploit business opportunities that present themselves as long as the associated risks are an appropriate and sustainable component of value creation. Risk management is a fundamental element of all business processes and decisions.

The targeted management of entrepreneurial opportunities and business risks alike is part and parcel of Lufthansa's corporate strategy. Consequently, the Company's system for the timely detection and management of risks consists of a multiplicity of components that are systematically embedded in the entire organisational and operational structure of the Company and its Group enterprises. There is no autonomous organisational structure; instead, risk management is regarded as a prime responsibility of the managers of all business entities and of the process and project managers in the Group companies. One of their management responsibilities is to ensure that the staff is likewise integrated into the risk management system.

The Risk Management Committee makes sure that risks are identified and assessed continuously across functions and processes. It is responsible for the system's constant further refinement and for verifying its effectiveness. It reports regularly to the Executive Board. The Committee further develops the basic principles of risk policy and oversees their compliance. It also communicates the Company's risk policy, defines the documentation requirements and initiates any necessary reviews of specific aspects of the risk management system by the internal auditing department.

All major potential risks to the Company's profitability or basis of existence are documented in a risk schedule; this risk schedule is regularly updated and extended. Major risks are defined as dangers which per se might cause damage equal to at least one third of the result necessary to maintain the Company's inherent value. Due account is taken of potential interdependencies between different risks.

The measures designed to ensure the timely detection, limitation and elimination of these risks within the framework of Lufthansa AG's risk management system are themselves regularly reviewed and reinforced. Over and above appropriate insurance solutions, countermeasures specific to each individual risk situation are envisaged to limiting and overcoming risks.

An analysis of risks, together with possibilities of limiting and overcoming them, also forms an integral part of the Company's strategy development process and is incorporated into Operational Group Planning.

The independent auditing company PwC Deutsche Revision AG carefully examined Lufthansa's system for the early detection of risks as part of its audit of the annual accounts. It confirmed that the system meets the defined requirements.

Risks and opportunities of future development

The effects of and fluctuations in global economic trends and the general macro economic settings have a fundamental impact on the Lufthansa Group's course of business development (Lufthansa, 2007).

Thus Lufthansa AG profited in 2004 from the global economic recovery, especially in long-haul traffic, where it carried 15.8 per cent more passengers and, despite a currency-related slight fall in yields, succeeded in fully placing the substantial extra capacity in the market and also in lifting the seat load factor. Lufthansa Cargo, too, was able to sell its extra available capacity of tonne-kilometres (+9.9 per cent) and to raise the sales volume by as much as 12.3 per cent, although at markedly lower average yields. A general economic slowdown, by contrast, usually tends to dampen demand in scheduled passenger business and also weakens the Lufthansa Group's business performance.

Opportunities for future development lie in particular in a speedy fall in fuel prices from the historic peak reached in 2004 and a resulting overall economic upturn. The Passenger Business, Logistics and Leisure Travel segments could profit from this.

Following the eastern enlargement of the EU, additional growth chances are also emerging in these regions, in which Lufthansa is already strongly represented, for the Passenger Business and Leisure Travel segments. All the business segments of the Lufthansa Group will be able to profit from the trend towards outsourcing of in-house production in response to the industry-wide cost pressures. Moreover, there is continuing strong pressure to consolidate in virtually all airline markets. The necessary consolidation process in Europe offers Lufthansa additional market opportunities thanks to its stable financial situation.

Competition

Competitiveness in the aviation industry, heavily dependent as it is on the cyclical development of the overall economy, hinges on how flexibly an airline can react to changes in demand and in the competitive environment. The introduction of further flexibility into fixed cost items is a crucial requirement for this and can be decisive for gaining a competitive edge. Staff costs have been made more flexible by the collective pay settlement concluded for ground staff and cockpit crews in December 2004 as part of the Concerted Action plan. This will enable the Company to react quickly to fluctuations in demand and to better equalise economic consequences. Competitive collective pay settlements specific to each individual business segment are necessary to enable the Company to keep pace on the cost front with other airlines, especially the no-frills carriers in Europe.

Lufthansa has adjusted further to the changed competitive setting on the production side, too. Thanks to the smoothing of the heaviest traffic flows (de peaking) at the Frankfurt and Munich hubs, both aircraft and staff productivity has been raised further. Lufthansa has thus laid the foundations for participating in the demand for attractively priced intra-European flights in the low-fare segment.

At the start of 2004 Lufthansa launched a comprehensive Action Plan, which enabled the Company to reduce costs by Euro 378m. One element of this Action Plan was the termination of the conventional commercial representative model of ticket distribution in many markets, including Germany, in favor of net pricing arrangements (zero commissions) with the distribution partners. The complaint filed by the German federation of travel agents and tour operators (Deutscher Reisebüro und Reiseveranstalter Verband e.V.-DRV) against the introduction of the net pricing model was withdrawn on 8 March 2005.

The safeguarding of profitable average yields requires offering business travellers a production and service profile which is recognizably far superior to the low-fare segment and meets their demands for a speedy ground service and comfortable and convenient flight conditions. Lufthansa has satisfied this requirement by upgrading the seat comfort of its Business Class product on long-haul routes with the new two-metre-long sleeper seat and on short-haul routes through the introduction of the four-seat row by leaving the middle seat vacant. Passengers in the long-haul segment also enjoy the globally unique facility of inflight broadband Internet access. With the introduction of the new service for HON Circle members and First Class passengers and the opening of the First Class Terminal in Frankfurt, Lufthansa offers its premium customers a new dimension in exclusive traveling.

Infrastructure

The planned extension of the runways at Frankfurt Airport is an important factor in Lufthansa's long-term competitiveness. The government of the state of Hesse (in which Frankfurt is situated) has likewise expressed its assent to an extension of the runway system following the clear recommendation given by the "mediation group" of independent experts. The extension project is a key precondition for securing Frankfurt Airport's future as an international air traffic hub. This applies equally to the construction of the maintenance hangar for the Airbus A380. The new super jumbo is in consequence of be deployed by Lufthansa from 2007 onwards. However, the operational restrictions that have meanwhile been introduced into the public debate on extending the airport would obstruct its efficient use. In particular, a practicable solution allowing a certain amount of night flights is crucial. If such a solution is not found, Lufthansa would have to partly refocus its flight schedule structure in the medium term on suitable alternative hubs.

Bottlenecks in the European air traffic control systems are continuing to cause substantial flight delays. The infrastructural shortcomings are burdening the profitability of all European airlines. In addition, they are jeopardizing the sector's ability to keep pace with the growing demand for air transport services. Together with other airlines, Lufthansa is therefore pressing the European Commission and the national governments to create an efficient system of air traffic control throughout Europe. Lufthansa has consistently underscored the importance of the infrastructural setting and has institutionalized this with the joint initiative "Air Traffic for Germany" with the respective partners - i.e. airports, air traffic control and public authorities.

Development of alliances

One of the mainstays of Lufthansa's commercial success is its integration into the world's leading airline partnership system, the Star Alliance. This summer it is offering its customers coordinated flight connections to 795 destinations in 139 countries. The loss-making situation in which many of the scheduled airlines worldwide at find themselves, has in the case of some of Lufthansa's partners, assumed proportions that threaten their existence. In December 2002 their key US partner United Airlines filed for protection from creditors with a view to restructuring under Chapter 11 of US insolvency law. Their Canadian partner Air Canada followed the suit on 1 April 2003 with a corresponding CCAA application under Canadian insolvency law. Whereas Air Canada successfully completed its restructuring process by 30 September 2004 and has achieved considerable improvements in its cost structure, United Airlines is still undergoing restructuring. Lufthansa is closely monitoring developments at United Airlines and is actively supporting its restructuring measures in an advisory capacity. On 12 September 2004 our second US Star Alliance partner US Airways reapplied for creditor protection under chapter 11 of US bankruptcy legislation. After US Airways had already sought creditor protection in the period from August 2002 to 1 April 2003, it emerged under the changed market environment, especially the fuel price trend, that the cost position of US Airways was not yet adequate to withstand competition. While the success of a restructuring of US Airways is uncertain, United Airlines - as the third largest US airline and having already achieved significant restructuring progress - appears to have a good chance of successfully completing the Chapter 11 procedure on a lasting basis. The termination of the restructuring procedure at United Airlines and a resumption of normal competitive operations are anticipated in the course of 2005. This would ensure a continuation of the transfer connections necessary in order to contribute to an extensive coverage of the key US market. Long-term close cooperation agreements have been signed with United Airlines and Air Canada which have been approved by the bankruptcy courts and largely ensure the exploitation of potential synergies.

Managing financial market risks

The hedging strategy to limit the risk of fluctuations in fuel prices, interest rates and exchange rates is laid down by the Executive Board of Deutsche Lufthansa AG. It is documented in internal guidelines which also provide for the use of derivative financial instruments. In this context interest rate and exchange rate hedges are also concluded with non-consolidated Group companies. Compliance with the guidelines is continuously monitored by the Group financial controlling and internal audit divisions. In addition, the current hedging strategy is constantly discussed in cross-division management committees. Appropriate management and control systems are in place for risk measurement, surveillance and control. The Supervisory Board is regularly informed of the exposure positions and the hedging results achieved.

Note 39 to the Consolidated Financial Statements of Deutsche Lufthansa AG gives a detailed account of the state of the exchange rate, interest rate and fuel price hedging operations.

Hedging fuel price risks

Each year the Lufthansa Group consumes about 6 million tonnes of kerosene. Fuel consumption thus constitutes a major cost item for the Group, just as it does for the entire airline industry. In the past financial year, it accounted for over 10.2 per cent of its total operating expenses; which is a marked increase over 2003. Large swings in fuel prices can have a significant impact on the result from operating activities.

The current fuel price-hedging strategy defines the maximum permissible level of the upward price risk, the maximum permissible outgoing payments from hedging transactions in the event of falling fuel prices, the maximum permissible premiums and the minimum degree of hedging. As a general principle, the price risk of up to 90 per cent of anticipated fuel consumption in the following 24 months is hedged on a revolving basis. The risk of unfavourable fuel price movements is primarily limited by hedges on the crude oil market. In addition, hedges are concluded on the price difference between gas oil and crude oil, kerosene and gas oil or directly between kerosene and crude oil, and in individual cases hedges are also concluded directly in gas oil or kerosene. At the reporting date crude oil hedges had been concluded for around 69.8 per cent of the anticipated fuel needs for 2005 in the form of corridor options and other hedging combinations. For 35.2 per cent of the hedged requirement for 2005 the effect of the hedge against price increases is limited by offsetting transactions to an average crude oil price level of approximately 41.7 USD/bbl. In addition, for 7.6 per cent of the anticipated fuel requirement for 2005 hedges have been concluded on the price differences between gas oil and crude oil and between kerosene and gas oil.

At the reporting date hedges had been concluded for around 3.7 per cent of the anticipated fuel requirement for 2006 in the form of other hedging combinations. In the case of such hedges the protection against rising prices is limited by counter-hedges to an average crude oil price level of around 49 USD/bbl.

If fuel prices in 2005 were to drop below the price level prevailing at the end of the year under review, this would significantly relieve Lufthansa's expenditure total. However, the associated potential cost relief will be partly limited by the put options written in the context of the hedging deals. Owing to the chosen hedging instruments, however, the price level of the put options is distinctly below that which prevailed at the end of 2004.

Hedging exchange rate risks

With respect to the US dollar, Lufthansa is a net payer, chiefly owing to its capital expenditure on aircraft. In line with the hedging strategy, 50 per cent of investments in aircraft are hedged against exchange rate fluctuations, as soon as they have been firmly contracted. The other half is hedged in the light of expected market developments. At the end of 2004 the degree of hedging of aircraft investments was 84 per cent. The US dollar exposure from operating business is currently Euro 0.2bn and the degree of hedging likewise stands at 84 per cent.

In the case of all other currencies, there is generally a net surplus of incoming payments. The euro equivalent of the hedged currencies currently totals Euro 2.2bn. The main exposures are in the currencies pound sterling, Swiss franc, Japanese yen and Swedish krona. A maximum of 50 per cent of the currency exposures arising from the expected payment flows in the individual currencies is normally hedged for a period of 18 months. Both forward contracts and corridor options are used for hedging exchange rate risks.

Hedging interest rate risks

Lufthansa's hedging strategy provides for hedging up to 100 per cent of firmly contracted floating-rate liabilities against interest rate risks. The euro equivalent of the financial liabilities relevant for hedging currently totals Euro 3.3bn, 61 per cent of which is hedged against interest rate risks. Interest rate risks are hedged by means of interest rate swaps and cross-currency swaps. The cross-currency swaps simultaneously serve to eliminate the exchange rate risks arising from financing in foreign currencies.

Up to 50 percent of planned liquidity surpluses or shortages may be hedged for a maximum period of 24 months. The interest rate risk that prevailed in 2004 on account of a persistent liquidity surplus was partly hedged by forward rate agreements.

Further development of the hedging strategy

As part of the ongoing development of the risk management strategy, new hedging concepts were elaborated during the year under review which will be gradually implemented as of the 2005 financial year.

The further elaboration of the fuel price hedging strategy foresees that the system of specifying limits for the maximum permissible upward price risk, the maximum permissible payment outflows under hedges in the event of falling fuel prices and the maximum permissible premium payments is to be replaced by a benchmark-based management system oriented to a linear build-up of hedges over a period of 24 months. The specification of minimum degrees of hedging will be retained.

Exchange rate risks from planned operational exposures are to be hedged in the future, to the extent of 20 per cent in each case, through forward contracts concluded 24, 18, 12 and 6 months before the inflow or outflow of the payment in question. Under this hedging policy, payment flows that lie in the distant future will be hedged to a lesser degree than payment flows in the near future. This takes due account of the uncertainty of the future course of business. The average degree of hedging will amount to 50 per cent.

As hitherto, 50 per cent of the contract value of investments in aircraft will continue to be hedged as soon as the contract is signed. The remaining 50 per cent will be hedged, to the extent of 10 per cent of the future payment stream in each case, 24, 18, 12 and 6 months before the outflow of the payment in question.

The interest rate risk from financial liabilities is to be generally hedged in the future to the extent of 15 per cent. The remaining 85 per cent will be subject to variable interest rates. This will take due account of the twin goals of minimizing interest expenditure in the long term and of reducing the volatility of earnings. The hedging volume of 15 per cent has proven, following detailed analysis, to be the optimum percentage for Lufthansa under cost and risk aspects.

Liquidity

The intensity with which global economic and geopolitical crises, terrorism and epidemics can affect the airline industry highlights the risk of maintaining inadequate liquidity reserves. Lufthansa has further improved its sophisticated financial planning systems. Based on a multi-year plan and crisis simulations, the level of the liquidity reserves considered necessary, defined as cash reserves plus free credit lines, has been adjusted accordingly and to date has not fallen below this level.

In addition, a new financial reporting system has been introduced for all companies majority-owned by the Lufthansa Group which contains information on the actual financial status and expected payment flows of individual companies. The data are collated centrally according to a standardized structure. At the end of each month, all companies report their respective financial asset and liability positions. The financial status report allows inferences to be made concerning liquidity and the level of net debt/net assets. On top of this the Group companies submit a monthly plan of payment flows, broken down by currency, for a period of 18 months (in the future 24 months). This monthly revolving plan provides an up-to-date picture of the expected liquidity trend.

Capital market

Lufthansa has an outstanding degree of flexibility compared with other airlines in the choice and design of its financing strategy and has access to the global financial and capital markets. This flexibility is based on the Company's high credit standing and on a forward-looking financing policy.

Lufthansa's operational strength and an appropriate financial profile are the basis of the investors' confidence in the Company. This confidence is also reflected in the creditworthiness assessment of the rating agencies. Lufthansa is currently the sole European airline to enjoy investment-grade ratings. These are assessed by Standard&Poor's at "BBB" and by Moody's at "Baa2". Owing to its good credit standing, Lufthansa can choose between multiple financing alternatives at attractive terms. Lufthansa uses this flexibility in order to continuously optimize its financing portfolio. The choice of tools is designed to reduce financing costs while ensuring operational and financial flexibility. Thus the Lufthansa Group has a share of unencumbered aircraft in its fleet of currently more than 80 per cent which can be used always as collateral for aircraft financing. In addition, Lufthansa maintains a constant liquidity stock of at least Euro 2bn which cushions it against cyclical fluctuations and volatilities in the financing markets.

Over and above this, Lufthansa has long-standing banking relationships with numerous credit institutions. During critical situations in the past, these banks have proven to be reliable partners for Lufthansa irrespective of fluctuations on the capital markets.

Credit risks

The sale of passenger and freight documents is largely affected via agencies. These agencies are mostly connected to country-specific clearing systems. The creditworthiness of the agents is continuously reviewed by the respective clearing houses. The receivables credit risk of sales agents is relatively small owing to broad diversification.

Inter-airline receivables and payables are settled on a bilateral basis or via the International Air Transport Association (IATA) clearing house. The general net settlement method of offsetting all receivables and payables at monthly intervals leads to a marked reduction of debitor default risk. In individual cases a separate surety is demanded in the respective performance contract for other business. In the event of an airline bankruptcy under the US Chapter 11 proceedings or comparable insolvency arrangements in other countries, the risks are likewise limited. As a rule the airlines seeking protection from creditors applies to the bankruptcy court for an exemption which allows them to uphold existing business relationships. In the past this application for exemption has always been granted by the court, thus facilitating the continuation of the high-volume and mutually lucrative interline business. The granting of the exemption entails the unconditional payment of all existing receivables and a particularly stringent monitoring of the payment behavior during the restructuring phase. In the event of a negative decision by the bankruptcy court Lufthansa is entitled to cease all payments immediately.

Lufthansa concludes many different types of financial market transactions. The debitor default risk arising from financial market transactions is defined as the risk resulting from a potential default of the contracting business partner. The objective of the debitor limit system in use at Lufthansa is the permanent assessment and management of this default risk. It was approved by the Executive Board in the context of adopting the guideline for hedging interest rate and exchange rate risks and the guideline for hedging fuel price risks.

A maximum permissible risk is defined for each counterparty (as a rule bank and mineral oil companies). This is largely derived from the assessment of recognized rating agencies. The execution of hedging transactions in the case of mineral oil companies is mostly outsourced to subsidiaries which have no rating of their own. If no declaration of warranty is provided by the parent company, a maximum credit line of Euro 10m can be set for these enterprises.

Within the defined counter party limit, the trading units may conclude individual transactions, such as financial investments, foreign exchange, interest rate and fuel financial derivatives as well as leasing deals, directly with the counter parties. The degree of utilization of these counterparty limits through existing financial market transactions is computed and reported on each business day. Any exceeding of the limits triggers an escalation process during which the initiation of further measures is decided.

Insurance

Deutscher Luftpool, previously the main insurer of aviation risks for the Lufthansa Group, ended its underwriting activity at the end of 2003. Although this radically changed the insurance environment for covering these risks, the insurance policy was subsequently placed on the international aviation insurance market without any major problem.

Although the costs of insuring the fleet have been reduced, they remain at a high level. Insuring against terrorist risks remains a key concern. Ensuring comprehensive long-term coverage of this risk continues to require intense cooperation among international insurers and ideally also among the international community.

Group companies

Lower passenger volumes, a cutback in flight capacity and reductions in the inflight service by US airlines in the wake of the terror assaults of 11 September 2001 have also seriously harmed the airline catering business of the LSG Sky Chefs group. Owing to the ongoing crisis affecting the established airlines in the US, the anticipated recovery of demand for airline catering services there has not yet occurred. Despite further capacity cuts, including the closure of non-profitable kitchens, rigorous cost management and the successfully concluded sale last year of the loss-making Chef Solutions division, the LSG USA group still did not manage to break even in 2004. The new management is rigorously continuing the restructuring plan, which envisages further cost cuts both in the production and administrative units.

The uncertain economic situation in Germany that remained until mid-2004 together with the non-improvement of the situation on the labour market continued to burden the leisure travel business of the Thomas Cook group in the year under review. The re-introduction of the Condor brand and its positioning in the low-price segment, the revival of the Neckermann brand and the closure of unprofitable travel bureaux in the German sales market have contributed to the repositioning of the group and to a marked improvement in the operating result. In addition, measures led in all the group's divisions are assisting to improve the cost position. The result after taxes in 2003/2004 was depressed, however, by necessary unscheduled impairment losses relating to the group's equity interests in France. Although it was significantly better than in the previous year it was still negative.

3.2. Continental Airlines

The airline industry has been through more structural changes in the past decade than most. Steve Goepfert explains how Continental Airlines' internal audit department has met the risk challenges.

Since we started our formal risk assessment process in the mid-1990s, there's no question that the airline industry has evolved tremendously. As such, much like other industries, the assessment by internal audit to identify and evaluate the audit universe must continually evolve as well. In particular, the internal audit department at Continental Airlines, Inc. (USA) has developed several processes to evaluate risk in its auditing environment (Goepfert, 2006).

Often, the establishment of a risk assessment process is viewed as a highly sophisticated, an elaborate, delicate process which is difficult to implement. In turn, many entities find themselves searching for a perfect package to 'solve' the mysteries of development and ultimately never implement anything. While there is definitely no shortage of off the shelf tools that can be used that can provide all the bells and whistles (and those are wonderful), developing a risk assessment process to meet your needs is much more manageable than often considered.

Continental Airlines is the world's sixth-largest airline with service reaching five continents: Europe, North America, South America, Asia and Australia. Continental, together with ExpressJet and Continental Connection, has been more than 3,200 daily departures throughout the Americas, Europe and Asia, serving 151 domestic and 137 international destinations. In the mid to late 1990s when the airline was continually growing, the internal audit department realized it needed to formally identify which areas needed attention and the timing for those reviews, and needed a systemic way to identify. With annual revenues of around $15 billion, the internal audit department is comprised of 23 people who work to ensure effective and appropriate internal controls are in place.

The audit universe at Continental is primarily comprised of corporate audits, field audits, IT audits and regulatory and compliance audits. Additionally auditors are actively engaged in assisting with US Sarbanes-Oxley Act compliance as well as various other special projects. Determination of projects to be audited in any given plan year is based on a unique risk analysis for each area. Additionally, the department utilizes a four-tier rating scale to provide an overall assessment of the audited area: Outstanding, Good, Needs Improvement, and Unsatisfactory. This rating is included in its reporting to senior management and the audit committee and is incorporated into the overall risk assessment. Additionally, the department has a commitment to senior management and the audit committee that any audit resulting in a rating of "Needs Improvement" or "Unsatisfactory" will be re-visited within twelve or six months, respectively.

The making of the model

Corporate audits encompass the audits of the financial and operational divisions of the company. In the early 1990s the department used a cyclical approach to performing reviews with an emphasis on financial and accounting functions. Dollar value expended or generated by the area primarily drove the process and management requests were considered. However, the department realized that other risk areas remained outside the normal audit focus, and that the timing of audits didn't always correlate with the relative risk environment currently existing in the company (a large, well-run operational area might be audited more frequently, than a smaller, poorly run function).

The department developed a process to assess the risk of the financial and operational units by evaluating the financial, inherent and reputational risks of the company. This risk assessment includes analyzing the balance sheet and income statement for large dollar amounts; obtaining a detail hierarchy of the accounts and analyzing large budget variances and related explanations; identifying if the business unit is performed solely in-house or serviced by a third party vendor; discerning the likelihood of errors and strengths of controls associated with the unit; assessing prior audit results for the unit; ascertaining if a new area or major changes to an area have incurred; In addition, identifying areas impacting corporate image and regulatory compliance. The department also engages with management to understand their concerns and identifies current issues or 'hot button' items to identify the timing for which the audit should be performed (sooner versus later). Assessing these matters provides the department to place business areas in categories of high/low dollar impact and parallel that with a high/low risk tolerance factor to clearly bring forth areas of focus. This allows for both quantitative and qualitative analysis to be used in the risk determination.

Field audits represent the audits performed of the airport and city ticket offices, international administrative offices and cargo facilities of the company. In the early 1990s, the approach for examining Field locations was to utilize a five-year cycle to audit all locations. The approach focused on the size of the location (number of flights, number of employees and revenues generated) as to frequency of the exam in this five year cycle. Management "requests" for audits and/or "tips" on problem stations also influenced the locale selections. While we were identifying problem locales, we also noted that we were expending time auditing locations routinely that were well run, and some smaller sites had more issues, and yet were receiving fewer audit visits (using the size criteria).

The first step in adopting a risk process for field locations was identifying what attributes were consistent across each locale and the drivers that impacted the success or failure of the attribute. The department launched a collaborative task force comprised of the key constituents that own/managed the operations to provide input as well as obtaining input from the CFO, controller and external auditors. The determination was made that once the attributes and success and failure drivers were identified, the timing of which locale to audit would be based on this analysis.

The department identified nine key risk attributes to use as indicators for the assessment of the locale. The attributes were comprised of station size, last audit date, last management change, prior audit report rating, compliance with submitting inventory reports, promptness of remitting funds, promptness of submitting sales reports, magnitude of unreported sales (passengers flown for which the ticket sale was not located), and magnitude of discrepancies with local disbursements. For each of these areas criteria were established to determine a measure for the significance of the risk. A point value was assigned to reflect a higher value as a higher risk. This allowed for the department to quantify the total risk per location and locales with a risk rating above the mid-point were considered first for inclusion in the plan.

This systemic analysis of audit locales with the higher risk rankings actively provided us to do audits of high risk areas first and was successful in that operating management queried as to how we knew what field locations had problems. Further, the department has seen an overall reduction in average risk point values which has given us an unanticipated benefit of empirically discerning that the overall risk environment in the field has improved over time.

IT audits represent the audits performed on existing applications, new systems development, general security controls, business resumption planning and penetration controls.

In the mid-1990s, Continental experienced a huge growth in technology initiatives being deployed which resulted in numerous changes to the way divisions operated.

During this time the IT audits reviews were focused almost entirely on mainframes, existing applications and data centers. With this massive change in new system initiatives, the department realized we needed to be more proactive in looking at these projects as well as distributive processing changed our primary mainframe focus.

In order to proactively assess the risk environment, the department first needed to increase its IT auditor staffing. This provided for the department to have sufficient resources to meet the demand of the rapidly growing technology function. The IT audits manager then coordinated directly with the chief information officer as well as senior technology management to discern major existing applications and platforms, new application and system development and any concerns of risk in processes performed in individual business units.

Reviews of the company's internal accounting reports reflecting work-in-progress budgets and expenses were also performed to identify where the financial resources were being expended. Additional factors of risk then include the last time a system had been audited, the audit rating, and whether the system is managed in-house or externally. The department utilizes this information to identify both the potential dollar impact to the company as well as reputation impact if a system fails to work as planned in determining the timing for which the review will be performed. This process has been instrumental in allowing the department to perform timely audits of the most important existing applications while aligning the audit team to be engaged at the critical times during a new system development project.

Keeping the momentum

The methodology for how the data is accumulated for each of the attributes continues to evolve and improve as automated data gathering techniques are developed (data warehouses, internal website reporting, etc); today, we can maintain a rolling 12 month database of field risk factors that allows us to continuously monitor these attributes. Further, the department continually evaluates the relevancy of the factors and weights used to measure current risk factors and makes adjustments as necessary. Thus, there is never an end point to defining the framework, but the department sees that having set a structure to the assessment factors provides the platform for providing more efficient and effective audits. A sound process should provide for continual growth and innovative, impactful auditing.

Launching ahead

Having had the ability to spend years developing, redefining and refreshing our internal risk assessment process, we are well positioned as the company pursues its Enterprise Risk Management process. As we pursue this effort, the internal audit department is supporting the risk management group (which owns this effort) and the risk management project team in identifying the company's major external and internal risks, setting a risk appetite, and evaluating identified risks against established controls. This exercise will also assist the internal audit in incorporating additional risk areas into its annual audit plan to ensure a comprehensive review throughout the organization **(Steve Goepfert is staff vice president, internal audit, at Continental Airlines,** August 18, 2006*).*

3.3. Delta Airlines

Chris Duncan, managing director of the National Business Group of Marsh USA Inc., in Atlanta, Ga., and former chief risk officer of Delta Airlines, Inc., spoke at the October Enterprise Risk Management (ERM) Roundtable hosted by NC State's College of Management ERM Initiative. Over 100 business professionals attending the demonstration in which Duncan provided an overview of how ERM was launched at Delta following the terrorist attacks of September 11, 2001 (NC State's ERM Roundtable Series, 2005).

Driven by a desire to impact shareholder value and improve overall governance, Delta launched its ERM efforts by first focusing on a subjective evaluation of risks rather than building a risk analysis system using detailed quantitative approaches. As the first chief risk officer (CRO), Duncan worked on building a process that continued to push responsibility of managing risks to key leaders of Delta's core business functions, while at the same time bringing information about risks together at the enterprise level. The emphasis was on strengthening the consistency of communications about risks across key business functions, while at the same time facilitating a more holistic view of key risks threatening Delta's core strategies and reputation.

To accomplish this at Delta, Duncan pulled together a team of executives to serve as Delta's Enterprise Risk Council (the ERC). These executives included leaders from Delta's safety, security, legal, internal audit, treasury, controller, and information security functions.

The primary task of the ERC was to oversee Delta's enterprise-wide view of risks and coordinate key risk oversight functions and to strive towards early identification of key risks threatening the enterprise. This group met monthly, while Duncan as CRO met quarterly with the chief financial officer and twice annually with the audit committee to discuss key risk exposures.

As CRO, Duncan worked with the ERC to map key risks affecting these core categories of business operations:

- Financial
- Operational
- Compliance
- Legal
- Security
- Human Capital
- Technology
- Political
- Reputation

As risks were identified, Duncan and the ERC mapped those risks based on the risks' likelihood and consequence. Consequence was ranked ordered based on these subjective evaluations:

- Survival Bet – the most severe consequence – the survivability of Delta is threatened.

- High
- Medium
- Low

Likelihood was assessed along these dimensions:
- The lottery – extremely hard to predict
- High
- Medium
- Low

Building on his experiences of leading Delta's ERM function from 2001 through 2004 and his experiences in leading risk management initiatives at Frito Lay and Kentucky Fried Chicken, Duncan offered these insights about critical success factors in any ERM effort:

- There must be clear ownership and accountability of risks across the organization (the CRO can't be the owner and or accountability person for risks – core business line leaders must be designated as the risk owner).

- The entity must have realistic expectations of success of risk control plans.

- Be aware leaders tend to over-estimate the effectiveness of a response to manage risks – executives need to be conservative in the assessment of residual risks (e.g., risks remaining after a response is implemented).

- The priority should be on closing key risk gaps for risks with the highest likelihood and consequence, particularly those that threaten the entity's survivability.

- Risk management must be integrated into financial planning (e.g., budgeting) and human capital processes (e.g., compensation).

- The entity's leaders must ensure that there is a process of ongoing communications about risks.

- Governance leaders within the enterprise must continually re-rank risks and identify new ones on an ongoing basis.

In his closing remarks, Duncan noted that "ERM is ultimately about changing culture and behavior and driving decision making and measurable results." He also said that "ERM is a matter of future survivability" and that getting ERM underway is more important than trying to develop the most sophisticated risk management system at the start. In essence – "just start."

3.4. Finnair Risk Management

Risk management at Finnair is part of the Group's management activity and is directed primarily at risks that threaten the fulfilment of the Group's business objectives. To exploit business opportunities, Finnair is prepared to assume managed and considered risks, taking the company's risk-bearing capacity into account. In contrast, in flight safety matters, for example, Finnair does not take risks.

In Finnair, risk management means a systematic and predictive way of analyzing and managing the opportunities and threats associated with operations. Risks are classified into strategic, operational, financial and accident risks. Risk management methods have been standardized for the recognition and classification of the Finnair Group's risks.

Organisation of risk management

The Board of Directors and the President & CEO are responsible for the Group's risk management strategy and principles as well as for the management of risks that threaten the fulfilment of strategic objectives. The President & CEO is responsible for ensuring that risk management is in other respects appropriately organized. The Senior Vice Presidents of the business units and the Managing Directors of subsidiaries are responsible for risk management in their own areas of responsibility.

Finnair Plc's Executive Board, which acts as a risk management steering group, assesses and directs risk management in Finnair Group. The company's internal auditing coordinates the reporting of risk management as well as adherence to a specified operating model.

The Flight Safety and Quality Departments, which operate under Finnair Plc's Accountable Manager, as specified in the Airline Operator's Licence, regularly audit the company's own and subcontractors' actions that impact on flight safety.

Operating environment risks

Demand and the price level of passenger and cargo traffic have been influenced most by global economic cycles, competition in the industry as well as various unexpected events, such as terrorism, environmental accidents and epidemics. The company has plans of action to minimize the operational impacts arising to air transport from various external disruptive factors.

The current trend clearly indicates that competitiveness in the air transport sector depends on how flexibly the company can react and adapt to unexpected events, changes in demand and a constantly changing competitive environment.

A critical factor for operational flexibility is the adjustment of fixed costs to fluctuations in demand. Moreover, the company's ability to react quickly in adjusting capacity, routes and costs to correspond to changing demand and economic and security conditions is also an essential factor in maintaining the company's profitability. In recent years Finnair has implemented, and has under way, a number of projects that have increased structural flexibility.

The European Union has a made proposal that air transport should join the emissions trading system as of 2011. Finnair considers emissions trading as a good starting point for controlling the environmental impact of air transport. The emissions trading scheme under the proposal is not considered to pose a significant financial risk to Finnair, due, among other things, to the company's environmentally positive fleet.

Finnair will defend its operating rights

An airline registered in the European Union can operate freely within the entire area of the Union. To date Finland, like other European countries, has been accustomed to negotiating bilateral operating agreements with countries outside the European Union.

In the future, regulation at the European Union level will bring the negotiation of aviation agreements between countries inside and outside the European Union under the European Commission. Existing bilateral operating agreements will remain in force in the new situation.

As a negotiating party the Union is stronger than an individual country and thus can strengthen the position of European airlines when negotiating operating rights. In some cases this may have an adverse impact on Finnair and may weaken the company's competitive position in relation to other European airlines. Finnair will actively strive to influence the parties who negotiate operating rights in order to safeguard its interests.

The company's operations are subject to legislative changes, to regulations and to changes in airport charges and taxes both on a national and an international level. The company actively monitors possible changes and strives to influence them via airline industry bodies, such as IATA and the Association of European Airlines (AEA).

Market risk

The air transport business is sensitive to both cyclical and seasonal changes. Competition in the sector is intense and the market situation is continually changing, which has reduced average ticket prices over an extended period. Airlines are cutting their prices in order to increase volumes, achieve sufficient cash flow and maintain market share.

Finnair constantly makes market situation analyses and actively monitors competitors' changes in pricing and capacity. Finnair is able to react quickly to pricing changes that take place in the market by utilising its advanced yield management systems for passenger and cargo traffic.

A change of one percentage point in the average price level of scheduled passenger traffic services affects the Group's operating profit by more than 10 million euros. Correspondingly a change of one percentage point in the load factor of scheduled passenger traffic services also affects the Group's operating profit by more than 10 million euros.

Finnair manages the residual value risk related to aircraft ownership by leasing approximately half of the aircraft belonging to its fleet under operating lease agreements of different durations. The leasing of aircraft also provides an opportunity for flexible capacity control in the short and long term.

Reliability of flight operations

Reliability is an essential prerequisite for operating successfully in the airline industry. The air transport business, however, is exposed to various disruptive factors, such as delays, exceptional weather conditions and strikes. As well as their impact on operational and service quality, air traffic delays also increase costs.

Finnair invests continually in the overall quality and punctuality of its operational activities. The Network Control Centre (NCC) gets together all the critical parties for flight operations, thus enabling the most effective overall solutions to be implemented. Finnair Technical's service punctuality and diverse expertise as well as its detailed specification of technical functions ensure the reliability of flight operations.

Furthermore, in operational activities the contribution of partners and interest groups is essential. Finnair monitors the quality of external suppliers within the framework of standards specified in advance and through regulations prescribed for flight operations.

According to statistics compiled on European network airlines, the arrival punctuality of Finnair's flights declined in 2006 compared with previous years. The company is still among the best airlines in the European (FORGOT A forpunctuality for, however.

In relation to Asian traffic, the transfer of passengers and goods from one flight to another at Helsinki-Vantaa Airport is increasing, in the short term, the risk of delays, owing to the airport's space restrictions. The completion of a new terminal extension in September 2009 will assist the situation considerably.

Risk of loss or damage

Management of risks relating to loss or damage is divided into two main areas: flight safety and corporate security. Development work in these areas is coordinated by the flight safety department and the corporate security unit. Risk management in this area encompasses, for example, risks to flights, people, information, property and the environment as well as liability and loss-of-business risks, and insurance cover. The priority in the management of risks relating to loss or damage is on risk prevention, but the company prepares for any possible emergence of risks through effective situation-management preparedness and insurance. Aircraft and other significant fixed assets are insured at fair value at least. The amount of insurance cover for aviation liability risks exceeds the minimum levels required by law.

Finnair actively monitors the effects of the company's operations on energy consumption, emissions and noise values. Finnair publishes annually a separate Environmental Report, which includes measures and key figures for the assessment of environmental efficiency.

Operational risk

Finnair's operations are based on a rigorous flight safety culture, which is maintained through continuous and long-term flight safety work. The company has prepared an operational safety policy, for which the company's Vice President, Flight Permits and Operating Licences is responsible for implementing. Every subcontractor working directly or indirectly with the Group's employees or flight operations must undertake to comply with the policy.

When operational decisions are made, flight safety always has the highest priority in relation to other factors that influence decision-making . Flight safety is an integral mechanism of all activities as well as a required way of operating not only for the company's own personnel, but also for subcontractors.

The main principle of flight safety work is non-punitive reporting of incidents in the way intended by the Aviation Act and the company's guidelines. The purpose of reporting is to find causes, not to assign blame. The company, however, does no tolerate wilful acts contrary to guidelines, methods or prescribed working practices. Decision-making not directly related to operations must also support the company's aim of achieving and maintaining a high level of flight safety.

Finnair is IOSA registered. The IOSA programme is an evaluation method for airlines' operational management and control systems. The audit which is the basis of IOSA registration states that an airline's operations fulfil the requirements of the IOSA standard.

Accident risk

The management of occupational health and safety is diverse and challenging, because the Finnair Group's operations are spread across many fields of business. Occupational safety risks are known to be high in precisely those areas - services, food industry, heavy aircraft maintenance, warehousing and transport - of which Finnair's operations principally consist.

The development of occupational safety is long-term work, and Finnair's goal is zero accidents. The investment in occupational safety made during 2006 has led to a positive trend in terms of accident frequency in nearly all of the Finnair Group's business units.

Means of improving occupational safety include identifying and evaluating safety hazards in the workplace and preventing accidents and hazardous situations. All reported incidents and accidents are investigated.

Telecommunications and technical risk

The diverse use of information technology in support of operations is increasing. Systems vulnerability and the development of new global threats represent a risk factor in a networked operating environment. Finnair is continually developing its information security and situation-management preparedness for serious disruptions to information systems and telecommunications. Such preparations have a direct impact on information technology and data security costs.

Developing information system solutions and the IT environment requires continuous investment. Careful selection of external partners in IT solutions also reduces the technology risk. The Group has gained access to technological expertise through, for example, cooperation with IBM.

Principles of financial risk management

The nature of the Finnair Group's business operations exposes the company to foreign exchange, interest rate, credit and liquidity, and fuel price risks. The policy of the Group is to minimize the negative effect of such risks on cash flow, financial performance and equity.

The management of financial risks is based on the risk management policy approved by the Board of Directors, which specifies the minimum and maximum levels permitted for each type of risk. Financial risk management is directed and supervised by the Financial Risk Steering Group. The implementation of financial risk management practice has been centralised in the Finnair Group's Finance Department.

In its management of foreign exchange, interest rate and jet fuel positions the company uses different derivative instruments, such as forward contracts, swaps and options.

3.5. Austrian Airline Risk Management

In the dynamic environment of the airline industry, active management of business risks and targeted identification and usage of opportunities count as part of daily commercial life for the Austrian Airlines Group. The Group's cross-department, value-oriented risk management system continuously records and analyses the trend in factors including exchange rates, interest rates, fuel prices, the load factor, yields and production costs. The management process was placed on a new footing in November 2006, and is now to be expanded further and developed into a Group-wide risk and opportunity management system

(http://www.austrianairlines.co..at/eng/Investor/Governance/Risk/, 2007).

As an aviation company, Austrian Airlines acts in a high-risk, dynamic environment. Risks and opportunities are part of everyday business life for the company. For some time now, Austrian Airlines has been working to actively manage its business risks. A department dedicated to risk management throughout the company has been in existence since the financial year 2003.

Group-wide, value-oriented risk management is now the responsibility of a single risk manager at Austrian Airlines. This individual will use institutionalized processes to continuously gather in and analyses all relevant risks, creating a basis for the prompt planning and implementation of countermeasures.

There is a particular focus on the proactive management of external factors, especially exchange rate, interest rate and fuel price trends.

Market risks mainly impact the load factor (capacity utilized) and yield (revenue per sold kilometer). Precise analyses of the respective booking situation allow for active revenue management oriented towards ongoing optimization.

Since the production of an airline (available kilometers) can only be adjusted to a limited extent in the short term, forward planning and scheduling, as well as the ability of a company to resist crises through flexibilisation of fixed costs, are of crucial importance. For this reason, the Group uses capacity management to match the "production" of flight services with current demand as precisely as possible and makes every possible effort to ensure excess capacity is usefully employed or sold. For the purposes of the Austrian Airlines Group quality offensive, a high level of transparency becomes particularly important. The ability to recognize risks early on, successfully control and manage these and to identify and use opportunities is absolutely central to the success of the offensive. It was with this in mind that the Group created a new Risk and Opportunity Management unit in November 2006, putting the management process of this area on a new footing. Step by step, the existing risk management will now be expanded further and developed to become a company-wide risk and opportunity management capable of making a valuable contribution to the overall management of the Group. The primary goal thereby is not so much risk avoidance as the controlled and conscious handling of risks and prompt recognition and realization of opportunities that present themselves.

3.6. Silverjet Risk Management

The airline industry faces a number of risks in today's climate, and as a start-up airline, they will not only be exposed to these industry-wide risks, but also to a number of other risks relating to our size. At Silverjet they take the pro-active management of these risks very seriously (this section source: http://www.flysilverjet.com/risk-management.aspx, http://www.flysilverjet.com/documents/FinalAdmissionDocument.pdf, **Accountants Report,** Deloitte & Touche LLP, 8 May 2006.).

Silverjet is a start-up company offering to operate a new basis of intercontinental long haul travel. At the time of receiving its financing, it will have no commercial contracts or regulatory approvals for operating. Silverjet's passengers will travel for business related and leisure reasons. As a substantial portion of such airline travel is discretionary, the airline industry tends to experience adverse financial results during economic downturns. It is possible that silverjet will be adversely affected by any downturn. Silverjet's business would also be adversely affected by any other circumstance getting a decrease in demand for air transportation services in or from the UK, the US and, in due course, elsewhere, in general, and business class traffic in particular. This includes adverse changes in local economic conditions, political disruptions or violence (including terrorism), fare increases linked to increased costs including increases in airport access costs or taxes imposed on air passengers and fuel costs, changes in business and leisure travel or spending patterns or other circumstances. The Directors intend that silverjet maintains a high aircraft utilization rate by virtue of its long haul route network. Silverjet's aircraft utilization may be adversely affected by delays resulting from factors such as air traffic control, ground handling, air traffic or airport congestion, weather, acts or negligence of third parties upon whom silverjet relies, maintenance and technical issues and other factors. Significant delays in silverjet's provision of services, especially if repeated on multiple occasions, could damage its reputation. Adverse effects may be further exacerbated to the extent silverjet regularly makes refunds and provides assistance to passengers if flight delays extend beyond four hours. In addition, silverjet's expansion of its network to include new bases, new destinations and more frequent flights on initial routes could be disruptive to silverjet's overall schedule, to the extent such expansion increases silverjet's exposure to congested airports or air traffic. The Directors plan that silverjet's overall capacity (measured in aircraft) will grow by 400 per cent over the first three years of operation. For a variety of reasons, silverjet may not be able to grow its business at the rate necessary to make sufficient use of this new capacity and avoid the adverse financial effects of having acquired too much capacity. Growth could be hampered by an economic downturn, problems specific to the air passenger industry or the business class portion of the industry, competitor action, air traffic or airport congestion, shortages of key or specialized personnel, availability of aircraft and other equipment, factors adversely affecting utilization, yields or load factors, changes in consumer preferences or other risks described in this section. Although the Directors think in the scalability of silverjet's business, expansion will place strains on silverjet's resources, including management, specialist personnel, information technology, internal controls and other resources.

Silverjet's management structure is deliberately lean; the Company may face shortages in pilots and other specialist staff, and its financial, control and planning systems will have to grow in complexity. Any shortfall in resources might require silverjet to make significant additional expenditures, including in respect of systems, facilities and personnel. An inability to hire the required personnel, or delays in designing and implementing effective new systems or the inability to acquire the necessary facilities or other assets might adversely affect silverjet's ability to develop in a cost-effective manner. In addition, the Board intends that silverjet will establish a highly cost-conscious and dynamic culture. These cultural values may be difficult both to create and to retain as silverjet grows.

Silverjet is face with the cost-effective management of new aircraft deliveries and deployments. The precise timing of aircraft deliveries can be affected by many factors over which silverjet have no control. Strategy of Silverjet for continued growth is dependent on its ability to acquire additional aircraft. The availability of aircraft is subject to market forces which can change swiftly, leading to strong movements in the lease or delivery costs of aircraft. In order to finance the acquisition of additional aircraft, the Directors intend that silverjet will enter into leasing arrangements which will mean a significant increase in the total amount of aircraft payment obligations to which silverjet will be subject. In the case of debt or lease finance, there can be no assurance that lenders or counter-parties will be available to silverjet at the times needed and with financing packages at affordable costs. In the case of aircraft held under lease, such leases cannot generally be terminated by silverjet without substantial financial penalty. If growth in passenger numbers and revenues do not keep up with the planned expansion of silverjet's fleet, silverjet could face difficulties meeting its aircraft payment obligations. Silverjet's failure to secure satisfactory agreements and relationships with its airport bases in the UK, the US and in due course elsewhere would have a significant impact on its ability to offer the type of service planned for its customers. Airport charges represent a significant operating cost to silverjet. Failure to secure contracts for satisfactory landing charges and handling and access agreements could also adversely impact the financial projections. In addition to the application of competition law at EU and national levels, the UK base from which silverjet will operate is specifically regulated. This means that all users of airports are required by law to be treated in a non-discriminatory manner and therefore the ability of silverjet or any other operator to negotiate preferential terms does not exist or is substantially restricted. At the airports where it has been permitted and has proven possible, silverjet will seek to negotiate the best arrangements it can make without regard to the arrangements made by other users of those airports.

In Europe, airports subject to particular congestion is regulated by a system of historical precedence in relation to slot allocation. Airports subject to slot allocation is known as "fully co-ordinated airports". Although London Luton Airport is not yet fully co-ordinated, it may become subject to various operating restrictions, including curfews, limits on aircraft noise levels, limits on the number of average daily departures and runway restrictions. These restrictions may limit silverjet's ability to continue to provide or to increase services at London Luton Airport. In addition, there is no assurance that airports at which there are no such restrictions may not implement some or all of these restrictions in the future, or that where such restrictions exist, they will not become more onerous.

Potential shortages of specialized personnel.

Pilots have at times been in short supply in the European airline industry and silverjet will have to expend significant time and effort to recruit and retain them. As pilots have an industry-customary three month notice period and new pilots take on average six months to recruit and train, there is a time gap that can be difficult to manage in recruiting and retaining pilots. Pilot shortages and the difficulties of managing new pilot staffing will be exacerbated for silverjet during silverjet's fleet expansion. Similar employment issues exist for licensed engineers, even though a proportion of these will be employed by silverjet's engineering provider.

Silverjet will be relatively small in size.

In comparison to other airlines, including some of its competitors, silverjet will have substantially fewer aircraft. If aircraft is unavailable for service on account of the need for repairs or for other reasons (other than routine maintenance), any resulting interruption in service could materially and adversely affect silverjet's business, financial condition and operation. The limited number of aircraft and routes intended by the Directors to be operated by silverjet means that silverjet will be less able than larger carriers to spread its operating costs over equipment and routes. Silverjet's ability to compete effectively with larger carriers may be adversely affected by its relatively small size.

Silverjet will be dependent on key personnel.

Silverjet's success will depend upon the efforts and abilities of its management team, including Lawrence Hunt, the Chief Executive, and John Bavister, the Finance Director, and other key financial, commercial and operating personnel including the postholders required for licensing purposes. Competition for highly qualified personnel is intense and the inability to recruit any of the proposed senior management of silverjet could lead to an adverse effect on its business, operating results and financial condition, especially if an adequate replacement cannot be found within a suitable time period.

Silverjet will be exposed to fuel price fluctuations, and increases in fuel costs or fuel shortages could materially affect operations.

Fuel costs constitute a substantial proportion of silverjet's total operating expenses and significant increases in fuel costs could materially affect silverjet's operating costs. Aircraft fuel costs have shown substantial volatility over the last few years. Both the cost and availability of jet fuel are subject to economic and political factors and events occurring throughout the world that silverjet can neither control nor accurately predict. Substantial price increases, such as those experienced in the last 12 months, or the unavailability of adequate supplies, could even lead, in extreme cases, to a curtailment of silverjet's scheduled services.

Silverjet has not entered into any hedging or other arrangements to provide against fluctuations in fuel prices and therefore silverjet is currently fully exposed to movements in fuel prices. The Company expects to enter into fuel hedging arrangements as soon as practicable.

Potential disruptions to business systems

Silverjet's ability to receive and process ticket purchases, manage reservations and its network, and engage in other critical business tasks will depend on the efficient and uninterrupted operation of its computer and communications systems. Contingency plans will be put in place to ensure that the reservations system could be brought back on-line within 24 hours in the event of major damage such as fire at the head office.

However, any significant disruption to silverjet's systems would damage the airline's ability to efficiently carry on its business. While silverjet will develop business continuity plans to cover all of its major systems and disruption a risk as soon as possible, a comprehensive plan is not currently in place.

Potential adverse impacts from new routes.

As silverjet acquires additional seat capacity, it intends to increase flight frequency on its existing routes, start new routes and ultimately establish new bases in its route network. To the extent silverjet is unable to expand its route network successfully, its future revenue and earnings growth may be limited and its financial strength may be reduced.

Silverjet will be dependent on third party service providers

The Directors intend that silverjet will enter into agreements with contractors for most of its aircraft maintenance needs: for the provision of crew, aircraft and insurance; for the implementation, maintenance and operation of its IT systems; for the provision of simulator time for training pilots; and for passenger and aircraft handling services, where it considers that such services can be more efficiently provided by third parties. Silverjet will attempt to obtain competitive rates for all such services by negotiating multi-year contracts at prices that are either fixed or subject to inflation-linked increases only. In addition, silverjet will seek to have unit rates reduced if levels of business increase markedly during the life of the contract. These contracts will normally be between one and ten years in length with termination at earlier dates by either party subject to suitable prior notice. There can be no assurance that silverjet will be able to get the necessary services at favorable rates.

Any inability to enter into these third party service contracts, or subsequently to renew them or to negotiate suitable replacement contracts, could result in an adverse effect on the Company. Although silverjet will seek to monitor the performance of third parties that provide it with maintenance and passenger and aircraft handling services, the efficiency, timeliness and quality of contract performance by third party providers will often be beyond silverjet's control. The Board expects silverjet to be dependent on third party arrangements for such services for the foreseeable future.

Government taxes may increase.

Airport taxes are levied as a fixed tax on the sale of air travel tickets in many of the countries in which the Directors expect silverjet to operate. The UK currently levies one of the highest air passenger taxes in Europe to points outside the EEA from within the UK. Regulators are currently considering the imposition of additional surcharges and taxes to reflect the environmental impact of aircraft operation.

Silverjet will be exposed to currency fluctuations

Silverjet will incur significant US Dollar denominated costs relating to aircraft to be leased pursuant to longterm operating leases, maintenance reserves, engine maintenance, aircraft fuel purchases, passenger handling services and marketing services. Silverjet's policy will be to hedge a proportion of its net US Dollar commitments in advance on a rolling basis. A significant portion of silverjet's revenue will be generated in US Dollars, however this is not expected by the Directors fully to offset the US Dollar denominated costs and accordingly silverjet is exposed to fluctuations in the value of the US Dollar against the pound until hedges are put in place. Further, a significant change in the proportion of US Dollar denominated revenue against expectations will leave silverjet exposed to unplanned fluctuations in hedged exposure, even within the rolling period referred to above.

Silverjet will be exposed to interest rate fluctuations.

The payments under any leases through which silverjet obtains its aircraft might be calculated by reference to a floating interest rate. As a result, silverjet's operational results and financial condition would be affected by fluctuations in the level of interest rates.

Silverjet may suffer from industrial action.

Silverjet will use some suppliers which are unionized and as such the airline may be negatively affected by industrial action outside its control. For example, some airport staff such as emergency fire service providers is union members. Should the relevant unions elect to take industrial action, for whatever reasons, the reliability of silverjet's operations could be compromised for extended periods of time. Furthermore, silverjet could also suffer from employee action from within silverjet once it has been launched. Although there is no intention to seek union recognition within silverjet, the Company will not be able to prevent this should employees seek it.

Risks related to Silverjet's Industry

Silverjet will operate in a competitive environment.

The level of competition among airlines is high. Airlines compete primarily on fare levels, frequency and reliability of service, brand recognition, passenger amenities and the availability and convenience of other passenger services. Most of the airlines with which silverjet will compete are larger and have greater name recognition and resources than silverjet. Some of these airlines have received, and may receive in the future, significant amounts of subsidies and state assistance from their respective governments. Some airlines are indeed so large, powerful or well-positioned that they can engage in anti-competitive activities in certain markets, with or without legal sanction. There can be no assurance that silverjet will be able to compete effectively against these airlines, any other industry members, or any new entrants to the industry.

The airline industry has been historically susceptible to fare discounting. This is partly in consequence of the typical airline cost structure, where there are very low marginal costs in respect of passengers occupying otherwise vacant seats. There can be no assurance that silverjet's competitors will not engage in price cutting activity or other changes in services in an effort to prevent silverjet gaining market share from them.

There are currently two other airlines offering business class only configurations similar to that which silverjet will offer, and there is no guarantee that other entrants will not seek to enter the market. Silverjet's business model is untested and open to competition. It is difficult to predict whether future head-to-head competition between silverjet and any other similar airline would be sustainable, when and where it may occur, or whether it would adversely affect silverjet.

Airlines are exposed to the risk of catastrophic loss.

Silverjet, like all airlines, will be exposed to the potential catastrophic losses that may be incurred in the event of an aircraft loss, accident or terrorist incident. Although silverjet will have adequate industry level insurance cover, there can be no assurance that the amount of such cover available in the event of losses from catastrophic events will not need to be increased, that insurance premiums will not increase significantly or that silverjet will not be forced to bear substantial losses from such events regardless of its insurance cover.

Any loss or accident relating to a silverjet aircraft, even if fully insured, could result in a loss in public confidence in silverjet as an airline and suspension or withdrawal of its licences. In addition, it may be that an aircraft accident relating to any other airline could result in a loss of public confidence in silverjet, to the extent that silverjet is perceived, rightly or wrongly, as conducting a similar business operation.

The airline industry is characterised by low profit margins and high fixed costs.

The airline industry is characterized by low profit margins and high fixed costs. The expenses of an aircraft flight do not vary significantly with the number of passengers carried and, therefore, a relatively small change in the number of passengers in relevant markets or in pricing, load factors or traffic mix could have a disproportionate effect on operating results.

Airline share ownership is restricted by national ownership requirements.

It is a requirement for all foreign carriers operating to the US to hold a foreign carrier permit from the FAA. In order to hold a foreign carrier permit a UK registered airline must be owned in the majority, and controlled, by UK nationals and not, as UK law requires, simply by EU nationals. The carrier must be able to demonstrate this at any time. Failure to do so may result in revocation of the carrier's operating licence. Accordingly, the Company's articles of association will give the Directors power to limit the ownership of the Company's shares by non-UK nationals and the ability to enforce this limitation. These constraints will continue to apply even if silverjet were to achieve a listing on any stock exchange at any time.

Risks related to Government regulation.

Granting and maintenance of silverjet's UK operating licences. Silverjet will be authorized to operate in the UK by virtue of an operating licence to be issued by the CAA. Following grant, the continuation of such authority is subject to ongoing compliance with applicable statutes, rules and regulations pertaining to the airline industry, including any new rules and regulations that may be adopted in the future.

Limitations on pilots and cabin crew working hours.. Under the UK CAA regulations, silverjet's pilots and crew will be subject to flight time limitations which may be varied from time to time. Silverjet intends to comply with these CAA regulations.

Risks related to the Ordinary Shares and the trading market.

As there has been no prior market for the Ordinary Shares, the Placing may fail to result in an active or liquid market for the Ordinary Shares, and the price of the Ordinary Shares may be highly volatile. Prior to the Placing, there has been no prior market for the Ordinary Shares. Although application has been made for the Ordinary Shares to be admitted to trading on AIM, an active public market may not develop or be sustained after the Placing. Active, liquid trading markets generally result in lower price volatility and more efficient execution of buy and sell orders for investors. If a liquid trading market for the Ordinary Shares does not develop, the price of the Ordinary Shares may become more volatile, and it may be more difficult to complete a buy or sell order for such Ordinary Shares. The trading prices of the Ordinary Shares may be subject to wide fluctuations in response to a number of factors, including:

• Fluctuations in the Company's operating results;

• Variations in national and industry growth rates;

• Actual or anticipated announcements of new services by the Company or its competitors;

• Changes in governmental legislation or regulation; or

• General economic conditions within the Company's business sector.

Future sales of shares may affect the market price of the shares.

Sales or the possibility of sales, of substantial numbers of Ordinary Shares in the public markets following the Placing could have an adverse effect on the market trading prices of the shares. The Company's subsequent equity offerings may reduce the percentage ownership of the Company's shareholders.

Detailed risks related to Silverjet

- **Silverjet will initially be dependent on the UK and North American travel markets** and any downturn in economic or political circumstances and/or increases in the cost of travelling could affect customer demand. As Silverjet will only take a relatively small market share of any route we operate on, Silverjet believe their low fares will enable Silverjet to continue to attract demand even during lean economic times.

- **Silverjet's low numbers of aircraft in the first few years will make us especially vulnerable to delays** if an aircraft experiences technical difficulties or faces extreme weather conditions. Silverjet has rigorous service recovery procedures in place, and in the event of a non-operational aircraft, Silverjet will book and pay for any affected customers to travel on other airlines.

- **Growth may be difficult to manage in a cost-effective manner** and Silverjet will incur significant costs acquiring new aircraft. Silverjet has a highly experienced management team, many of whom have worked for airlines - including Virgin and easyJet - who have also experienced rapid growth in aircraft numbers, as well as members of Silverjet's team who have worked for start-ups in other industries and are experienced in managing the transition from small to large organisations. Using Silverjet's experience combined with Silverjet's low cost ethos, they are believing Silverjet have a strong team in place which will control and manage this growth.

- **Potential shortages of specialised personnel** (such as pilots) may limit Silverjet's ability to grow. Silverjet already has a full complement of experienced pilots and inflight managers in place to launch its first aircraft and has been oversubscribed during recent recruitment for both pilots and cabin crew. Silverjet believes the strength of the Silverjet proposition will attract many more applicants once the airline is operational.

- **Silverjet will be exposed to fuel price fluctuations**, and increases in fuel costs or fuel shortages could materially affect operations. We recognize this is one of their largest financial exposures and plan to hedge Silverjet's fuel costs to limit this exposure. The Silverjet business plan was drawn up at the height of the recent fuel price increase and prices are now below their projected fuel costs.

- **Silverjet will be dependent on third party service providers**. The recent acquisition of Flyjet Limited has reduced one of the key dependancies, on a third party to provide Silverjet's aircraft operating certificate (AOC) and flight operations, by bringing this activity in-house and generating a significant cost saving over 5 years. All Silverjet's third party service providers have a lead member of the management team responsible for that relationship, and many of Silverjet's suppliers have a risk/reward element to their remuneration linking Silverjet's success to theirs.

- **Silverjet will be exposed to currency and interest rate fluctuations**. Silverjet plan to hedge, particularly in US dollars, to minimise this area of risk.

Risks relating to the Airline Industry

- **Silverjet will operate in a very competitive environment**. Silverjet has a very competitive proposition - 30 minute check-in through a private jet terminal, combined with a one touch flat bed and highly personalized service, for a very affordable price of £999 average return fare. Three years of customer research, planning and competitor analysis have gone into creating Silverjet and Silver Class, and while Silverjet expect some competitors to match some elements of Silverjet's offering, no single competitor can match all elements. Continuous innovation and a focus on constantly driving costs out of the business will enable Silverjet to react to competitor challenges and continually evolve Silverjet's business model to meet changing customer demands.

- **Airlines are exposed to the risk of catastrophic loss**. Silverjet will operate to the highest standards of safety and security and will act closely with all the relevant authorities to ensure that customer safety is paramount always .

- **The airline industry is characterised by low profit margins and high fixed costs.** Silverjet's business model will minimise fixed costs by outsourcing and/or sale and lease back of key cost areas, as well as utilising technology and new developments to drive costs out of the business moving forwards. This will enable Silverjet to operate from a low cost base to support a low fare, great value structure.

- **Airline share ownership is restricted by national ownership requirements.** Siverjet is proud to be a British airline and do not foresee national ownership requirements restricting the growth of Silverjet's business and their fleet.

3.7. JETBLUE

The competitive landscape continues to be ever-changing across the U.S. airline industry. Traditional airlines are revamping their cost structures and new "airline within an airline" concepts are being designed to compete directly against JetBlue. While limitation remains the sincerest form of flattery, JetBlue take these competitive challenges seriously and view them as opportunities to further improve their airline.

JetBlue Airways Corporation, or JetBlue, is a low-fare, low-cost passenger airline that provides high-quality customer service primarily on point-to-point routes. JetBlue focus on serving underserved markets and large metropolitan areas that have high average fares, and JetBlue have a geographically diversified flight schedule that includes both short-haul and long-haul routes. JetBlue intended to maintain a disciplined growth strategy by increasing frequency on their existing routes and entering new markets.

The airline industry is highly competitive and JetBlue expect competition to continue in the future. Recent adverse economic conditions continue to put pressure on the airline industry, with two of the 11 major U.S. airlines in bankruptcy. In addition, in response to the growth in the market share of low-fare airlines, several major airlines have announced initiatives to meet the growing demand of fare conscious travelers. JetBlue was incorporated in Delaware in August 1998.

The airline industry is highly competitive. Airline profits are sensitive to adverse changes in fuel costs, average fare levels and passenger demand. Passenger demand and fare levels have historically been influenced by, among other things, the general state of the economy, international events, industry capacity and pricing actions taken by other airlines. The principal competitive factors in the airline industry are fare pricing, customer service, routes served, flight schedules, types of aircraft, safety record and reputation, code-sharing relationships, in-flight entertainment systems and frequent flyer programs.

JetBlue's competitors and potential competitors include major U.S. airlines, low-fare airlines, regional airlines and new entrant airlines. The major airlines are larger, have greater financial resources and serve more routes than JetBlue do. Some of these competitors have chosen to add service, reduce their fares or both, in some of JetBlue's markets following their entry. They also use some of the same advanced technologies that JetBlue do, such as ticketless travel, laptop computers and website bookings.

The passenger airline industry in the United States has traditionally been dominated by the major U.S. Airlines, the largest of which are American Airlines, Continental Airlines, Delta Air Lines, Northwest Airlines, Southwest Airlines, United Air Lines and US Airways. The DOT defines the major U.S. Airlines as those airlines with annual revenues of over $1 billion, which currently consists of 11 passenger airlines. The major U.S. Airlines offer scheduled flights to most large cities within the United States and abroad and also serve numerous smaller cities. Most major U.S. Airlines have adopted the "hub and spoke" the route system . This system concentrates most of an airline's operations at a limited number of hub cities, serving most other destinations in the system by providing one-stop or connecting service through the hub. Regional airlines, such as Atlantic Coast Airlines and SkyWest Airlines, typically operate smaller aircraft on lower-volume routes than major U.S. airlines. In contrast to low-fare airlines, regional airlines generally do not try to establish an independent route system to compete with the major U.S. airlines. Rather, regional airlines typically enter into relationships with one or more major U.S. Airlines under which the regional airline agrees to use its smaller aircraft to carry passengers booked and ticketed by the major U.S. airline between a hub of the major airline and a smaller outlying city. Low-fare airlines largely developed in the wake of deregulation of the U.S. Airline industry in 1978, which permitted competition on many routes for the first time. There are three low-fare major U.S. airlines. Southwest Airlines, the largest low-fare, major U.S. airline, pioneered the low-cost model by operating a single aircraft fleet with high utilization, being highly productive in the use of its people and assets, providing a simplified fare structure and offering only a single class of seating. This enabled Southwest to offer fares that were significantly lower than those charged by other major U.S. airlines. During the 1980s, industry consolidation, rapid increases in multi-type aircraft fleets, increases in labor costs and development of the "hub and spoke" systems caused the cost structures of the major U.S. airlines to rise substantially. Although a number of low-fare airlines were created during the 1980s, primarily due to under capitalization or flawed business plans most of them eventually failed. In the early 1990s, the domestic airline industry suffered substantial financial losses in consequence of adverse economic conditions and reduced demand for air travel. The turmoil in the airline industry in the early 1990s made an opportunity for a new generation of low-fare airlines. Entrepreneurs capitalized on the availability of surplus aircraft, recently unemployed, experienced aviation professionals and airports with unused capacity.

While Southwest remains the largest low-fare airline today, other low-fare airlines have also been able to offer substantially lower fares than the major U.S. airlines. Low-fare airlines have been able to stimulate demand by attracting fare-conscious leisure and business passengers who might otherwise have used alternative forms of transportation or not traveled at all. As a result, low-fare airlines with an acceptable level of service and frequency have seen a migration of business travelers away from the major U.S. airlines. These trends have contributed to significant growth in the low-fare airline sector, with low fare airline market share doubling in the last five years to over 17% of domestic capacity.

The terrorist attacks on September 11, 2001, in which four U.S. commercial aircraft was hijacked and crashed, dramatically affected the airline industry. U.S. airlines have experienced numerous difficulties in the wake of these tragic events, including but not limited to, a significant drop in demand for air travel, reduced traffic and yields, increased insurance and security costs and liquidity concerns. As a result, several of JetBlue's East Coast competitors have reduced their capacity, including flights in JetBlue's current and potential markets. US Airways eliminated its MetroJet operation, which was designed to compete with low-cost, low-fare airlines, such as Southwest and us. Delta Air Lines significantly reduced the capacity of its Delta Express service, which was its low-fare, leisure-oriented service provider in the Northeast and Midwest to Florida. This has provided opportunities for us to introduce new service and increase JetBlue's number of flights between existing destinations. In November 2002, National Airlines ceased operations which resulted in us initiating JetBlue's New York-Las Vegas service earlier than originally planned. However, in response to the growing market share of low-fare airlines, several major airlines have announced initiatives to meet the increased demand of fare-conscious travelers. Delta Air Lines has announced the creation of a new low-fare subsidiary, which is intended to be more cost-competitive and provide a distinct brand and customer experience. It intends to offer simple, everyday low fares that are one-way and nonrefundable, starting initially on its Northeast to Florida markets. United Air Lines has also announced that it plans to create a separate low-cost airline to become more competitive in the leisure travel market.

Continuing adverse economic conditions have kept pressure on the airline industry. The major U.S. Airlines reported operating losses of $10 billion in each of 2001 and 2002. In response to these adverse financial results, some airlines have been reexamining their traditional business models and have taken actions in an attempt to increase profitability, such as reducing capacity, furloughing or terminating employees, limiting service offerings, attempting to renegotiate labor contracts and reconfiguring flight schedules in order to increase aircraft utilization, as well as other efficiency and cost-cutting measures. However, despite these business model adjustments, financial losses have continued and US Airways and United Air Lines filed for Chapter 11 bankruptcy on August 11, 2002 and December 9, 2002, respectively. Additional airline bankruptcies and restructuring may occur, potentially resulting in substantial change in JetBlue's industry, which could adversely affect JetBlue business.

Since deregulation of the airline industry in 1978, there has been continuing consolidation in the domestic airline industry. Further consolidation in the industry could result in a greater concentration of assets and resources among the major U.S. airlines. The more recent trend is the formation of marketing alliances. These alliances generally provide for code-sharing, frequent flyer program reciprocity, coordinated flight schedules that provide for convenient connections and other joint marketing activities. These alliances also permit an airline to market flights operated by other alliance airlines as its own. The benefits of broad networks offered to customers, such as the recently announced alliance between Northwest Airlines, Continental Airlines and Delta Air Lines, could attract more customers to these networks. JetBlue does not currently participate in any marketing alliances, which could harm JetBlue's competitive ability. JetBlue does not interline or offer joint fares with other airlines, nor do JetBlue have any commuter feeder relationships. The airline industry also faces competition from ground transportation alternatives. Video teleconferencing and other methods of electronic communication may contribute a new dimension of competition to the industry as business travelers seek lower-cost substitutes for air travel.

Risks Related to JetBlue

JetBlue's JetBlue's failure to successfully implemented JetBlue's growth strategy could harm JetBlue's business.

JetBlue's growth strategy involves increasing the frequency of flights to markets JetBlue currently serve, expanding the number of markets served, increasing flight connection opportunities and successfully establishing Long Beach Municipal Airport as JetBlue's West Coast base of operations. Achieving JetBlue's growth strategy is critical in order for JetBlue's business to achieve economies of scales and to sustain or increase JetBlue's profitability. Increasing the number of markets JetBlue serve depends on JetBlue's ability to access suitable airports located in JetBlue's targeted geographic markets in a manner that is consistent with JetBlue's cost strategy. Operating only one aircraft type, the A320, is cost-efficient, but it limits JetBlue's ability to fly to markets too small to support a 162-seat aircraft operation and add frequency to smaller markets. JetBlue will also need to obtain additional gates at some of JetBlue's existing destinations. Any condition that would deny, limit or delay JetBlue's access to airports JetBlue seek to serve in the future will constrain JetBlue's ability to grow. Opening new markets requires us to commit a substantial amount of resources, even before the new services commence. Expansion will also require additional skilled personnel, equipment and facilities. An inability to hire and retain skilled personnel or to secure the required equipment and facilities efficiently and cost-effectively may affect JetBlue's ability to achieve JetBlue's growth strategy. Other airlines have tried to establish a presence at Long Beach and have failed. JetBlue cannot assure you that JetBlue will be able to successfully expand JetBlue's existing markets or establish new markets, and JetBlue's failure to do so can harm JetBlue's business.

JetBlue has a significant amount of fixed obligations and JetBlue will incur significantly more fixed obligations which could hurt JetBlue's ability to meet JetBlue's strategic goals.

As of December 31, 2002, JetBlue's debt of $712 million accounted for 63.2% of JetBlue's total capitalization. All of JetBlue's long-term and short-term debt has been floating interest rates. In addition to long-term debt, JetBlue have a significant amount of other fixed obligations under operating leases related to JetBlue's aircraft, airport terminal space, other airport facilities and office space. As of December 31, 2002, future minimum lease payments under non cancelable operating leases with initial or remaining terms in excess of one year were approximately $290 million for 2003 through 2007 and an aggregate of $379 million for the years thereafter. As of

December 31, 2002, after reflecting a February 2003 amendment, JetBlue had commitments of approximately $1.86 billion to purchase 49 additional aircraft over the next five years, including estimated amounts for contractual price escalations. JetBlue will incur additional debt and other fixed obligations as JetBlue take delivery of new aircraft and other equipment and continue to expand into new markets. JetBlue typically financed JetBlue's aircraft through either secured debt or lease financing. JetBlue has arranged financing for JetBlue's first five deliveries scheduled for 2003.

JetBlue's high level of debt and other fixed obligations could:

• impact JetBlue's ability to obtain additional financing to support capital expansion plans and for working on capital and other purposes on acceptable terms or at all;

• divert substantial cash flow from JetBlue's operations and expansion plans in order to service JetBlue's fixed obligations;

• require us to incur significantly more interest or rent expense than JetBlue currently do, since all of JetBlue's debt has been floating interest rates and five of JetBlue's aircraft leases have variable-rate rent;

• place us at a possible competitive disadvantage compared to less leveraged competitors and competitors that have better access to capital resources.

JetBlue's ability to make scheduled payments on JetBlue's debt and other fixed obligations will depend on JetBlue's future operating performance and cash flow, which in turn will depend on prevailing economic and political conditions and financial, competitive, regulatory, business and other factors, many of which are beyond JetBlue's control. JetBlue cannot assure you that JetBlue will be able to generate sufficient cash flow from JetBlue's operations to pay JetBlue's debt and other fixed obligations as they become due, and JetBlue's failure to do so can harm JetBlue's business. If JetBlue is unable to make payments on JetBlue's debt and other fixed obligations, JetBlue could be forced to renegotiate those obligations or obtain additional equity or debt financing. To the extent JetBlue finance JetBlue's activities with additional debt, JetBlue may become subject to financial and other covenants that may restrict JetBlue's ability to pursue JetBlue's growth strategy.

Because JetBlue has a limited operating history, it is difficult to evaluate an investment in JetBlue's common stock.

JetBlue was incorporated in August 1998 and started flight operations in February 2000. It is difficult to evaluate JetBlue's future prospects and an investment in JetBlue's common stock due to JetBlue's limited operating history. JetBlue's prospects are uncertain and must be considered in light of the risks, uncertainties and difficulties frequently encountered by companies in the early stage of operations. Historically, there has been a high failure rate among start-up airlines. JetBlue's future performance will depend on JetBlue's ability to implement JetBlue's growth strategy, react to customer and market demands, maintain adequate control of JetBlue's expenses and maintain the safety and security of JetBlue's operations.

JetBlue's results of operations will fluctuate.

JetBlue expected JetBlue's quarterly operating results to fluctuate in the future based on changes in aircraft fuel and security costs and the timing and amount of maintenance and advertising expenditures. In addition, seasonal variations in weather and traffic affect JetBlue's operating results from quarter to quarter. The highest levels of traffic and revenue on JetBlue's routes to and from Florida are generally realized from October through April and on JetBlue's western routes during the summer. Given JetBlue's high proportion of fixed costs, this seasonality affects JetBlue's profitability from quarter to quarter. Many of JetBlue's areas of operations in the Northeast experience bad weather conditions in the winter, causing increased costs associated with deicing aircraft, cancelled flights and accommodating displaced passengers. JetBlue's r Florida routes experience bad weather conditions in the summer and fall as a result of thunderstorms and hurricanes. In consequence of JetBlue's geographic area of operations, JetBlue are more susceptible to adverse weather conditions along the East Coast than some of JetBlue's competitors, who may be better able to spread weather-related risks over larger route systems. As JetBlue enters new markets, JetBlue could be subject to additional seasonal variations.

In consequence of the factors described above, quarter-to-quarter comparisons of JetBlue's operating results may not be good indicators of JetBlue's future performance. In addition, it is possible that in any future quarter JetBlue's operating results could be below the expectations of investors and any published reports or analyses regarding JetBlue. In that event, the price of JetBlue's common stock could decline, perhaps substantially.

JetBlue's maintenance costs will increase as JetBlue's fleet ages.

Because the average age of JetBlue's aircraft is 15.5 months, JetBlue's aircraft require less maintenance now than they will in the future. JetBlue also currently incur lower maintenance expenses because most of the parts on JetBlue's aircraft are under multi-year warranties. JetBlue's maintenance costs will increase on an absolute basis, on a per seat mile basis and as a percentage of JetBlue's operating expenses, as JetBlue's fleet ages and these warranties expire. Although JetBlue cannot accurately predict how much JetBlue's maintenance costs will increase in the future, JetBlue expect that they will increase significantly.

If JetBlue are unable to attract and retain qualified personnel at reasonable costs or fail to maintain JetBlue's company culture, JetBlue's business will be harmed.

JetBlue's business is labor intensive, with labor costs representing 30.6% of JetBlue's operating expenses for the year ended December 31, 2002. JetBlue expect salaries, wages and benefits to increase on a gross basis and these costs could increase as a percentage of JetBlue's overall costs, which could harm JetBlue's business. JetBlue's expansion plans will require us to hire, train and retain a significant number of new employees in the future. From time to time, the airline industry has experienced a shortage of personnel licensed by the FAA, especially pilots and mechanics. JetBlue compete against the major U.S. airlines for labor in these highly skilled positions. Many of the major U.S. airlines offer wage and benefit packages that exceed JetBlue's wage and benefit packages. As a result, in the future, JetBlue may have to significantly increase wages and benefits in order to attract and retain qualified personnel or risk considerable employee turnover. If JetBlue are unable to hire, train and retain qualified employees at a reasonable cost, JetBlue may be unable to complete JetBlue's expansion plans and JetBlue's business could be harmed. In addition, as JetBlue hire more people and grow, JetBlue believe it may be increasingly challenging to continue to hire people who will maintain JetBlue's company culture. One of JetBlue's principal competitive strengths is JetBlue's service-oriented company culture that emphasizes friendly, helpful, team-oriented and customer-focused employees. JetBlue's company culture is important to providing high quality customer service and having a productive workforce that helps keep JetBlue's costs low. As JetBlue grow, JetBlue may be unable to identify, hire or retain enough people who meet the above criteria, and JetBlue's company culture could otherwise be adversely affected by JetBlue's growing operations and geographic diversity. If JetBlue fail to maintain the strength of JetBlue's company culture, JetBlue's competitive ability and business may be harmed.

JetBlue's failure to properly integrate LiveTV, LLC could harm to business of JetBlue.

On September 27, 2002, JetBlue acquired all the membership interests of LiveTV, a provider of in-flight entertainment, which is outside JetBlue's previous line of business. Acquisitions often involve risks, including:

• Difficulties in integrating the operations, technologies, products and personnel of LiveTV;

• Diversion of management's attention from normal daily operations of the business;

• The potential loss of key employees of LiveTV;

• Inability to maintain consistent standards, controls, policies and procedures; and

• Insufficient experience in entering into new product or technology markets.

JetBlue's failure to properly integrate the operations of LiveTV could harm JetBlue's business.

JetBlue's failure or inability to enforce JetBlue's patents could harm JetBlue's business.

One of the unique features of JetBlue's fleet is the free live television JetBlue provide at every seat which was developed by LiveTV, which JetBlue now own. JetBlue has certain federal patents which are important to maintaining JetBlue's competitive position in providing this unique product to JetBlue's customers in-flight. Therefore, JetBlue intends to devote the appropriate resources to the protection of JetBlue's proprietary rights over this developed technology. The protective actions that JetBlue takes may not be enough to prevent imitation by others, which could harm JetBlue's business. Although JetBlue is not aware of anyone else who has developed comparable live satellite TV technology, Delta has announced that, in conjunction with Matsushita Avionics Systems, it intends to provide a similar product to Delta's new low cost subsidiary by October 2003. Matsushita or others may succeed in these efforts without violating JetBlue's patent rights or intellectual property.

JetBlue may be subject to unionization, work stoppages, slowdowns or increased labor costs.

Unlike most airlines, JetBlue have a non-union workforce. If JetBlue's employees unionize, it could result in demands that may increase JetBlue's operating expenses and adversely affect JetBlue's profitability. Each of JetBlue's different employee groups could unionize at any time and require separate collective bargaining agreements. If any group of JetBlue's employees was to unionize and JetBlue were unable to reach agreement on the terms of their collective bargaining agreement or JetBlue were to experience widespread employee dissatisfaction, JetBlue could be subject to work as slowdowns or stoppages. In addition, JetBlue may be subject to disruptions by organized labor groups protesting JetBlue's non-union status. Any of these events would be disruptive to JetBlue's operations and could harm JetBlue's business.

JetBlue's lack of a marketing alliance could harm JetBlue's business.

Many airlines have marketing alliances with other airlines, under which they market and advertise their status as marketing alliance partners. Among other things, they share the use of two-letter flight designator codes to identify their flights and fares in the computerized reservation systems and permit reciprocity in their frequent flyer programs. JetBlue is not a member of any marketing alliance. JetBlue's lack of a marketing alliance could harm JetBlue's business and competitive ability.

If JetBlue failed to comply with financial covenants, some of JetBlue's financing agreements may be terminated.

Under some of JetBlue's financing agreements, JetBlue are required to comply with specified financial covenants. JetBlue cannot assure you that JetBlue will be able to comply with these covenants or provisions or that these requirements will not limit JetBlue's ability to finance JetBlue's future operations or capital needs. JetBlue's inability to comply with the required financial maintenance covenants or provisions could result in a default under these financing agreements and would result in a cross default under JetBlue's other financing agreements. In the event of any such default and JetBlue's inability to obtain a waiver of the default, all amounts outstanding under the agreements could be declared to be immediately due and payable. If JetBlue did not have sufficient available cash to pay all amounts that become due and payable,

JetBlue would have to seek additional debt or equity financing, which may not be available on acceptable terms, or at all. If such financing was not available, JetBlue would have to sell assets in order to obtain the funds required to make accelerated payments or risk JetBlue's aircraft becoming subject to repossession, which could harm JetBlue's business.

JetBlue is subject to the risks of having a sole supplier for JetBlue's aircraft, engines and a key component of JetBlue's in-flight entertainment system.

One of the elements of JetBlue's business strategy is to operate only one type of aircraft equipped with one type of engine. After extensive research, JetBlue chose the Airbus A320 by reason of its reliability, advanced technology and wide cabin space and the IAE International Aero Engines V2527-A5 engine for its reliability and fuel efficiency. JetBlue's dependence on a single type of aircraft and engine for all of JetBlue's flights makes us particularly vulnerable to any problems associated with the Airbus A320 or the IAE V2527-A5 engine, including design defects, mechanical problems or adverse perception by the public that would result in customer avoidance or an inability of us to be able to operate JetBlue's aircraft. If either Airbus or IAE were unable to perform its contractual obligations, JetBlue would have to get another supplier for JetBlue's aircraft or engines. Boeing is the only other manufacturer from whom JetBlue could purchase alternate aircraft. If JetBlue had to purchase aircraft from Boeing, JetBlue could lose the benefits described above and JetBlue cannot assure you that any replacement aircraft would have the same operating advantages as the Airbus A320. In addition, JetBlue cannot assure customer that JetBlue could purchase engines that would be as reliable and efficient as the V2527-A5, or that JetBlue could purchase aircraft or engines in the same time frame as currently expected or at comparable prices. JetBlue would incur substantial transition costs, including costs associated with retraining JetBlue's employees and replacing JetBlue's manuals. JetBlue's operations could also be harmed by the failure or inability of Airbus or IAE to provide sufficient parts or related support services on a timely basis.

One of the unique features of JetBlue's fleet is that every seat in each of JetBlue's aircraft is equipped with free LiveTV, a direct 24-channel satellite TV service. An integral component of the system is the antenna, which is supplied to us by EMS Technologies, Inc. JetBlue do not know of any other company that could provide us with this equipment and if EMS were to stop supplying us with its antennas for any reason, JetBlue could lose one of the unique services that differentiates company from JetBlue's competitors, and JetBlue might have to incur significant costs to procure an alternate supplier.

JetBlue's business is heavily dependent on the New York market and a reduction in demand for air travel in this market would harm JetBlue's business.

JetBlue's growth has focused and, at least in the near-term, will continue to focus, on adding flights to and from JetBlue's primary base of operations at JFK in New York City. As of February 14, 2003, out of a total of 180 daily flights, 146 of JetBlue's flights had JFK as either their destination or origin. As a result, JetBlue remain highly dependent upon the New York market. JetBlue's business would be harmed by any circumstances causing a reduction in demand for air transportation in the New York metropolitan area, such as adverse changes in local economic conditions, negative public perception of the city, significant price increases linked to increases in airport access costs and fees imposed on passengers or the impact of past or future terrorist attacks.

If JetBlue fail to use certain airport slots and slot exemptions, JetBlue may be required to forfeit these slots and the deposits JetBlue paid to hold them.

The DOT granted us 75 daily takeoff and landing slot exemptions at JFK in 1999. A slot is an authorization to take off or land at a designated airport within a specified time period. Unlike a slot, JetBlue's exemption from slot authorization requirements may not be sold, leased, rented or pledged. These slot exemptions phased in at the rate of up to 25 daily slots per year over three years ending in February 2003. If JetBlue fail to maintain JetBlue's use of a slot exemption, such slot exemption could be subject to forfeiture. Since JFK is JetBlue's principal base of operations, JetBlue's failure to maintain JetBlue's slot exemptions at JFK could harm JetBlue's business. In May 2001, the City of Long Beach granted us the 27 remaining available daily non-commuter departure slots at Long Beach Municipal Airport. JetBlue currently use 18 slots and must use all of the slots by June 2003 or the unused slots and the deposits associated with them will be forfeited. Until such time as JetBlue use slots that were allocated to us, JetBlue's slots remain available for other carriers to use on a temporary basis. American Airlines has requested and been granted temporary use of four of JetBlue's slots by the City of Long Beach. In addition, a request by Alaska Airlines for three slots was denied. Settlement negotiations are presently underway among the parties and JetBlue cannot assure you that JetBlue will be able to maintain all of JetBlue's slots.

JetBlue may face increased competition at JFK which could harm JetBlue's business.

JetBlue's primary base of operations is JFK, an airport that has traditionally attracted considerably less attention from JetBlue's competitors for domestic flight activity than either LaGuardia Airport or Newark International Airport because of an industry perception that JFK is primarily an international airport and that the commuting distance from Manhattan to JFK is too far to attract domestic travelers. JetBlue disagreed with this perception of JFK and believe that the operational efficiencies associated with conducting JetBlue's principal base of operations from JFK have contributed to JetBlue's profitability. As a result of JetBlue's positive experience at JFK, it is possible that JetBlue's competitors will follow JetBlue's strategy. Airlines already established at JFK could increase their existing presence at JFK with a greater emphasis on low-fare domestic travel. One example is Delta's recent announcement to launch a low-fare airline service which intends to provide non-stop service from all three New York area airports, including JFK, to key Florida leisure markets. Other airlines that do not currently have a presence at JFK could try to gain a presence at JFK by seeking slot exemptions from the DOT as JetBlue did or purchasing or leasing slots from other airlines. In addition, airlines using fewer than 20 slots or providing regional jet service to small and medium, non-hub airports could easily obtain slot exemptions from the DOT, since such airlines are expressly exempted under the federal rule creating slot restrictions. The requirement to obtain slots or slot exemptions at JFK will expire in 2007, further opening the door to potential competition. In addition, gates are available at JFK, which could create more opportunities for JetBlue's competitors to increase or establish their presence at JFK. An increase in the amount of direct competition JetBlue face at JFK, LaGuardia or Newark, or an increase in congestion and delays at JFK could harm JetBlue's business.

JetBlue may be unable to renew or replace JetBlue's permit at JFK, JetBlue's principal base of operations.

JetBlue currently operate from Terminal 6 at JFK under an expired permit from the Port Authority of New York and New Jersey. JetBlue's permit could be terminated at any time upon 30 days' notice and alternate gate space may not be available on favorable terms, or at all. Although JetBlue are in the process of finalizing a long-term lease agreement through November 2006 with the Port Authority, JetBlue cannot assure you that JetBlue will be able to execute a lease agreement. Since JFK is JetBlue's principal base of operations, JetBlue's inability to maintain an adequate number of gates would harm JetBlue's business.

JetBlue's business could be harmed if JetBlue lose the services of JetBlue's key personnel.

JetBlue's business depends upon the efforts of JetBlue's Chief Executive Officer, David Neeleman, JetBlue's President and Chief Operating Officer, David Barger, and a small number of management and operating personnel. JetBlue maintain key-man life insurance on Messrs. Neeleman and Barger, which may not be sufficient to cover the costs of recruiting and hiring a replacement chief executive officer or president, much less the loss of their services. JetBlue may have difficulty replacing management or other key personnel who leave and, therefore, the loss of the services of any of these individuals could harm JetBlue's business.

JetBlue's employment agreements with JetBlue's FAA-licensed personnel provide that JetBlue can only terminate these employees for cause and, as a result, it may be difficult to reduce JetBlue's labor costs during an economic downturn, which could harm JetBlue's business.

JetBlue's employment agreements with JetBlue's FAA-licensed personnel, including pilots, technicians and dispatchers, provide that these employees can only be terminated for cause. Each employment agreement is for a term of five years and automatically renews for an additional five-year term unless either the employee or JetBlue elect not to renew it by giving notice at least 90 days before the end of the initial term. In the event of a downturn in JetBlue's business, JetBlue are obligated to pay these employees a significant portion of their employment income and to continue their benefits if they do not obtain other aviation employment. As a result, it may be difficult for company to reduce JetBlue's labor costs during an economic downturn, and JetBlue's inability to do so could harm JetBlue's business.

JetBlue's lack of an established line of credit or borrowing facility makes us highly dependent upon JetBlue's operating cash flows.

JetBlue have no lines of credit, other than a short-term borrowing facility for certain aircraft predelivery deposits, and rely primarily on operating cash flows to provide working capital. Unless JetBlue secure a line of credit, borrowing facility or equity financing, JetBlue will be dependent upon JetBlue's operating cash flows to fund JetBlue's operations and to make scheduled payments on JetBlue's debt and other fixed obligations. If JetBlue fail to generate sufficient funds from operations to meet these cash requirements or are unable to secure a line of credit, other borrowing facility or equity financing, JetBlue could default on JetBlue's debt and other fixed obligations. JetBlue's inability to meet JetBlue's obligations as they become due would materially restrict JetBlue's ability to grow and seriously harm JetBlue's business and financial results.

JetBlue's inability to obtain approval to operate more aircraft from the FAA and the DOT would materially restrict JetBlue's growth.

JetBlue must obtain the approval of the FAA and the DOT to operate aircraft domestically. JetBlue currently have approval from the FAA and the DOT to operate 40 aircraft through May 2003. JetBlue's growth plans and aircraft purchase commitments contemplate operating considerably more than 40 aircraft. JetBlue have submitted an application to the DOT for authorization to increase the size of JetBlue's fleet beyond 40 aircraft. This application will be based on a demonstration of JetBlue's financial and managerial fitness and safety compliance for expanded operations. The failure of the FAA and the DOT to grant us approval to operate additional aircraft would materially restrict JetBlue's ability to grow and to increase revenues and cash flow.

Risks Associated with the Airline Industry

The airline industry tends to experience adverse financial results during general economic downturns and recent airline financial results may lead to significant changes in JetBlue's industry.

Since a substantial portion of airline travel, for both business and leisure, is discretionary, the industry tends to experience adverse financial results during general economic downturns. The airline industry has been experiencing a decline in traffic, particularly business traffic, due to slower general economic conditions beginning in 2000 and more recently, from the lingering impact of the terrorist attacks of September 11, 2001. The industry experienced record losses for the year ended 2001 and the major U.S. airlines reported net losses of more than $11 billion in 2002. In response to these adverse financial results, some airlines have been reexamining their traditional business models and have taken actions in an effort to increase profitability, such as reducing capacity and rationalizing fleet types, furloughing or terminating employees, limiting service offerings, attempting to renegotiate labor contracts and reconfiguring flight schedules, as well as other efficiency and cost-cutting measures. However, despite these business model adjustments, financial losses have continued and US Airways and United Air Lines filed for Chapter 11 bankruptcy protection in 2002. Additional airline bankruptcies and restructurings may occur, potentially resulting in substantial change in JetBlue's industry, which could adversely affect JetBlue's business.

The 2001 terrorist attacks seriously harmed JetBlue's industry and the increased risk of additional attacks ormilitary involvement in Iraq, the Middle East or other regions may harm JetBlue's industry in the future.

The terrorist attacks of September 11, 2001 and their aftermath have negatively impacted the airline industry. The primary effects experienced by the airline industry included substantial loss of passenger traffic and revenue, increased security and insurance costs, increased concerns about future terrorist attacks, airport delays due to heightened security, and significantly reduced yields due to the drop in demand for air travel. Industry-wide demand for air travel has increased but has not yet returned to pre-September 2001 levels.

Additional terrorist attacks, the fear of such attacks, increased hostilities or military involvement in Iraq, the Middle East or other regions could negatively impact the airline industry, and result in further decreased passenger traffic and yields, increased flight delays or cancellations associated with new government mandates, as well as increased security, fuel and other costs.

Increases in fuel costs would harm JetBlue's business.

Fuel costs constitute a significant portion of JetBlue's total operating expenses (14.4% for the year ended December 31, 2002). Significant increases in fuel costs would harm JetBlue's financial condition and results of operations. JetBlue estimate that for 2002, a one cent increase in the price per gallon of fuel expense would have increased JetBlue's fuel expense by $1.06 million. Historically, fuel costs have been subject to wide price fluctuations based on geopolitical issues and supply and demand. Fuel availability is also subject to periods of market surplus and shortage and is affected by demand for both home heating oil and gasoline. Because of the effect of these events on the price and availability of fuel, the cost and future availability of fuel cannot be predicted with any degree of certainty. In the event of a fuel supply shortage, higher fuel prices or the curtailment of scheduled service could result. Some of JetBlue's competitors may have more leverage than JetBlue do in obtaining fuel. JetBlue cannot assure you that increase in the price of fuel can be offset by higher fares. In addition, although JetBlue implemented a fuel hedging program in 2001, under which JetBlue enter into crude oil option contracts to partially protect against significant increases in fuel prices, JetBlue's fuel hedging program does not protect us against ordinary course price increases and is limited in fuel volume and duration.

Airlines are often affected by factors beyond their control, including weather conditions; traffic congestion at airports and increased security measures, any of which could harm JetBlue's operating results and financial condition.

Like other airlines, JetBlue are subject to delays caused by factors beyond JetBlue's control, including adverse weather conditions, air traffic congestion at airports and increased security measures. Delays frustrate passengers, reduce aircraft utilization and increase costs, all of which negatively affect profitability. During periods of fog, snow, rain, storms or other adverse weather conditions, flights may be cancelled or significantly delayed. Cancellations or delays due to weather conditions, traffic control problems and breaches in security could harm JetBlue's operating results and financial condition.

Changes in government regulations imposing additional requirements and restrictions on JetBlue's operations could increase JetBlue's operating costs and result in service delays and disruptions.

Airlines are subject to extensive regulatory and legal requirements, both domestically and internationally, that involve significant compliance costs. In the last several years, Congress has passed laws, and the DOT and the FAA have issued regulations relating to the operation of airlines that have required significant expenditures. JetBlue expect to continue to incur expenses in connection with complying with government regulations. Additional laws, regulations, taxes and airport rates and charges have been proposed from time to time that could significantly increase the cost of airline operations or reduce the demand for air travel. If adopted, these measures could have the effect of raising ticket prices, reducing revenue and increasing costs.

The airline industry is characterized by low profit margins and high fixed costs, and JetBlue may be unable to compete effectively against other airlines with greater financial resources or lower operating costs.

The airline industry is characterized generally by low profit margins and high fixed costs, primarily for personnel, aircraft fuel, debt service and rent. The expenses of an aircraft flight do not vary significantly with the number of passengers carried. As a result, a relatively small change in the number of passengers or in pricing could have a disproportionate effect on an airline's operating and financial results. Accordingly, a minor shortfall in expected revenue levels could harm JetBlue's business. In addition, the airline industry is highly competitive and is particularly susceptible to price discounting because airlines incur only nominal costs to provide service to passengers occupying otherwise unsold seats. JetBlue currently compete with other airlines on all of JetBlue's routes. Many of these airlines are larger and have greater financial resources and name recognition or lower operating costs or both than JetBlue do. Some of these competitors have chosen to add service, reduce their fares or both, in some of JetBlue's markets following JetBlue's entry. Therefore, JetBlue may be unable to compete effectively could harm JetBlue's business.

JetBlue's insurance costs have increased substantially as a result of the September 11th terrorist attacks and further increases in insurance costs would harm JetBlue's business.

Following the September 11th terrorist attacks, aviation insurers dramatically increased airline insurance premiums and significantly reduced the maximum amount of insurance coverage available to airlines for liability to persons other than passengers for claims resulting from acts of terrorism, war or similar events to $50 million per event and in the aggregate. In light of this development, under the Stabilization Act, the government has provided domestic airlines with excess war risk coverage above $50 million up to $3.0 billion per event. In December 2002, via authority granted to it under the Homeland Security Act of 2002, the government expanded its insurance program such that airlines could elect either the government's excess third-party coverage or for the government to become the primary insurer for all war risks coverage. While the Homeland Security Act of 2002 authorized the government to offer both policies through August 31, 2003, the current policies are in effect until April 14, 2003. It is expected that should the government stop providing war risk coverage to the airline industry; the premiums charged by aviation insurers for this coverage will be substantially higher than the premiums currently charged by the government. Significant increases in insurance premiums would harm JetBlue's financial condition and results of operations.

Substantial consolidation in the airline industry could harm JetBlue's business.

In recent years, and particularly since its deregulation in 1978, the airline industry has undergone substantial consolidation, and it may undergo additional consolidation in the future. Recent economic conditions and airline financial losses may contribute to further consolidation within JetBlue's industry. Any consolidation or significant alliance activity within the airline industry could increase the size and resources of JetBlue's competitors, which, in turn, could adversely affect JetBlue's ability to compete.

JetBlue's reputation and financial results could be harmed in the event of an accident or incident involving JetBlue's aircraft.

An accident or incident involving one of JetBlue's aircraft could involve repair or replacement of a damaged aircraft and its consequential temporary or permanent loss from service, and significant potential claims of injured passengers and others. JetBlue is required by the DOT to carry liability insurance. Although JetBlue believes JetBlue currently maintain liability insurance in amounts and of the type generally consistent with industry practice, the amount of such coverage may not be adequate and JetBlue may be forced to bear substantial losses from an accident. Substantial claims resulting from an accident in excess of JetBlue's related insurance coverage would harm JetBlue's business and financial results. Aany aircraft accident or incident, even if fully insured, could cause a public perception that JetBlue are less safe or reliable than other airlines, which would harm JetBlue's business. [Source: JETBLUE AIRWAYS CORP (Form: 10-K/A, 03/08/2005)].

CHAPTER V

THE BEST ERM OPERATOR IN THE AIRPORT BUSINESS

CHAPTER V

THE BEST ENTERPRISE RISK MANAGEMENT OPERATOR IN AIRPORT BUSINESS

"The Best ERM Operator Selection in Airport Business"

1. INTRODUCTION

In today's uncertain business environment, ERM has become the new management strategy for risk management executives and airport business managers. By managing the risks in the enterprise-wide concept, organizations achieve greater gains and competitive advantages in their industry. In this business environment, managers and board members demand a deeper understanding of how risk is being managed in their business and how to manage risk to purposely make the greatest reward for their shareholders. Risk prioritization is the key element in this concept.

ERM is separated from traditional risk management approaches in terms of focus, objective, scope, emphasis and application. ERM aligns strategy, people, processes, technology and knowledge. The emphasis is on strategy, and the application is enterprise-wide. ERM is a response to the sense of inadequacy in using a silo-based approach to manage increasingly interdependent risks. The discipline of ERM is a more robust method of managing risk and opportunity and an answer to business pressures. ERM is also designed to improve business performance.

The underlying premise of ERM is that; every entity, whether for-profit or not, or for a governmental body, exists to provide value for its stakeholders. All entities face with uncertainty, and the challenge for management is to determine how much uncertainty the entity is prepared to accept as it strives to grow stakeholder value. Uncertainty presents both risk and opportunity, with the potential to erode or enhance value. ERM offers a framework for management to effectively deal with uncertainty and associated risk and opportunity and thereby enhance its capacity to build value (COSO, 2004).

Airport business risks are greater today than ever, like any other businesses. ERM implementation is a necessity to airport business. The study is aimed to support current ERM efforts in the airport business. This study is also aimed to contribute to ERM literature regarding to the airport business. The range of current literature about airport business ERM is very narrow.

ERM provides a framework for management to effectively deal with uncertainty and associated risk and opportunity and thereby enhances its capacity to build value. ERM is used for optimization of risk and opportunity. One of the most critical challenges for management today is determining how much risk the business is prepared to accept as it strives to create value. At this point, critical importance of risk prioritization appears. This chapter is prepared to offer a new approach to select the best ERM operator.

This chapter recommends an application of the analytic network process (ANP) for the selection of best operator for enterprise risk management (ERM) in the airport business. This survey deals with solving "Who has the best practices reasonably linked to the ERM Implementation in the airport business?" problem. In order to determine the best practice criteria to the ERM, interview with airport managers is experienced and best practice surveys and ERM guidelines are analyzed. ERM is basically needed for serious investment, resources and integrated holistic approach. The complex concept mentioned above, many various criteria have importance for best ERM implementation. ANP used to solve the problem, includes many measure and interdependency. TAV Airport Holding Co. and Fraport A.G. are determined to be alternatives in the proposed ANP model. Also, Fraport AG and TAV Airport Holding Co. are selected as samples of the real world situation in this research.

Recent developments and changes in the airport business environment have completely changed both the risks organizations face and their management of those risks. Globalization, e-business, new organizational partnership, changes in the air transportation industries and the increasing speed of business activity are rapidly changing and expanding the organisations face. ERM has emerged as an important new business trend at the airport business environment. ERM is structured and disciplined approach aligning strategy, process, people, technology and knowledge with the use of evaluating and managing the uncertainties the enterprise faces as it creates value. "Enterprise-wide" means the removal of traditional functional, divisional, departmental, or cultural barriers. A truly holistic, integrated, future-focused, and process-oriented approach generously serves an organization manage all key business risks and opportunities with the intent of maximizing shareholder value for the enterprise as a whole. Business leaders are realizing that risk creates opportunity that opportunity creates value, and that value ultimately creates shareholder wealth. "How best to manage risks to derive that value?" has become the critical question. ERM has the potential to provide organisations with a new competitive advantage (Mercer Oliver Wyman, 2006).

ERM is a worthy goal for all businesses, regardless of size. Risk-management activities need to be tied to strategy and ultimately built into everyday business processes (Crowe Chizek and Company LLC, 2006). This is valid also for airport business.

Airports are vital gateways for developing local business, and as such are a key component of local, national and regional infrastructure. At the same time, airports are much more than regulated public service providers. They are complex commercial entities that must meet well-defined business objectives in terms of day-to-day operations, financial performance and planning for future growth (ACI, 2006). To realize the complexity of airport business, many factors need to be taken into consideration: traffic growth, capacity, competition, financial results, revenue streams, employment, capital expenditure, ownership, relations with airlines, the regulatory environment and aviation industry cooperation (ACI, 2006).

The some unchanging fundamentals are to the airport business. First, society becomes prosperous through the flow of people and goods. Airports are and will continue to be the engine of economic growth. Second, the airport business is a business of risk management. Today, airports have to maximize the social and economic value to stakeholders. Airport managers have to manage their airport by more systematic and holistic approach. They have redefined the airport business: it's not just a place to board and disembark passengers or load and unload cargo; it's the center of integrated multi-modal flows of people, goods, information and capital. They are not just considering about air transport; air, sea and land feed into each other, and their job is to integrate that to gain maximum advantage for society and their selves. The airport of the 21st century needs to reach out to the source of the flow, to understand the marketplace and to see solutions to meet the needs of its customers (Pang, 2004).

Today's airport business is dynamic, competitive, complex, and unpredictable. The context of the airport operator, especially in market-oriented, wealthy environments, is changing rapidly. Illustrations of this development are the privatization drive of airports, the effects of liberalization and deregulation of the air transport market on airports (as experienced to the extreme cases of the bankruptcies of Sabena and Swissair), upcoming new entrants into the airport business, and last but not least the demanding societal requirements for acceptable effects of airports on their neighbors. This all means that long term strategic planning for airports is more complex than ever. However, an airport cannot sustain itself without a long-term vision and strategy. The stakeholders associated with airports are changing as well. The main new stakeholder, especially for privatized airports, is the financial market, which sets new requirements on financial performance (Wijnen, 2003). This increasingly complex and dynamic set of circumstances motivates the need for ERM implementation. ERM is a fundamental part of strategic planning and all managerial efforts in the airport business. For these reasons, ERM is a must for airport business in today's world; that's to say it is not optional.

The art of managing risk is more challenging than ever. ERM has become a focus point in the air transportation industry and airport business like the other business and industries. In today's business environment, managers are focused on the question how the best ERM should be practiced. Most organizations are uncertain about how, exactly, to translate the concept of ERM into concrete action steps that will gradually help their best practice. Rather, there is an emerging consensus about how to achieve the effective ERM implementation and how the organization can benefit from the ERM. In this study, I deal with solving "who is the best operator about ERM implementation in the airport business?" problem. Best practice criteria that affect the best practice of ERM by performing literature searches and analysis of ERM framework guidelines, case study and ERM survey reports are determined. TAV Airport Holding Co. and Fraport A.G. are selected as alternatives in the ANP model. These alternatives can be assessed according to the strategic, operational and financial criteria. As a result of this model application, one of them is selected as the best alternative regarding to ERM implementation. However, many extra efforts will be required to be the best in the ERM concept. For this reason, many suggestions are developed in the conclusion part of this chapter.

Analytic Network Process (ANP) methodology is used in this chapter. ANP provides a more generalized model in decision-making without making assumptions about the independency of the higher-level elements from lower-level elements and also of the elements within a level. Despite all these merits, the applications of ANP are not very common in a decision-making problem. However, in recent years, there has been an increase in the use of ANP in multi-criteria decision-making problems. In the selection of the best ERM operator, the criteria are of both subjective and objective types. These criteria also have some interdependencies, which cannot be captured by the popular AHP method. Therefore, instead of using the commonly used AHP approach for solving such types of problems, I recommend the use of an ANP-based model for the selection of a best operator.

The objective of this chapter is to introduce a comprehensive decision methodology for the selection of a best operator that airport managers can consider in their implementations about ERM. The proposed methodology allows assessment and benchmarking of alternative operators. Also, this chapter gives relevant information about the best practice of ERM. Following questions are responded in this chapter:

- What are ERM and the best ERM practice?
- What are the best practice criteria?
- What should be done for the best ERM implementation in airport business?

In this chapter ANP serves as the decision analysis tool, and i implemented it using Super Decisions, sophisticated and user-friendly software that implements ANP (Saaty, 2001a). ANP makes it possible to deal systematically with the interactions and dependencies among the factors in a decision system (Bayazit and Carpak, 2007). The criteria are based on the results of literature search and analysis of guidelines published by various organizations about ERM framework. Furthermore, in this chapter, I mentioned the ANP methodology and explained the criteria considered to affect the best practice of ERM. The criteria of best ERM practice for airport business are listed and divided into three main groups such as strategic, operational and financial. The reason of this division is the purpose of shaping according to the ANP approach.

2. THE ENTERPRISE RISK MANAGEMENT TO AIRPORT BUSINESS

Air transportation industry is one of the world's most important industries. Air transportation plays a vital role in developing and facilitating economic growth, particularly in developing countries like Turkey. Airports, as key factors of production of air transport, are directly influenced by what happens to the industry. Development and changes in the air transportation such as deregulation, liberalization, privatization, commercialization, and competitive structure, have an influence over airports which are critical and fundamental elements of the air transportation system.

ERM is important in airport business. Airports are and will continue to be the engines of economic growth. Airports are fundamental elements of an air transportation system. In addition, airport business practices play a critical role in shaping airline competition. Development and changes in the air transportation such as deregulation, liberalization, privatization and commercialization, and competitive structure, influence the airports which are a part of air transportation system. These developments and changes have important consequences in planning, design, and management of airports. Uncertainty and risks are increase as a consequence of these developments and changes. ERM implementation is essential for survival of airport business. In the air transportation sector, airports, air traffic control facilities, and government airlines become more commercial-oriented and have been partially or fully privatized in many circumtances.

Airlines and airports face challenging in dynamic market environments that in the short term are extremely sensitive to the world economic and political situation. Airport business practices play a critical role in shaping airline competition (FAA/OST Task Force Study, 1999). Uncertainty and risks are increasing and driving as a result of this development and changes. So, ERM guides for survival of airport business.

Commercialized and privatized airports are improving and increasing in terms of service concepts, quantity and network in the world-wide. This trend indicates the rapid development of airport business. This process is risky and risks must be managed. Air transportation and airport businesses have more risks than any other industries. These risks appear suddenly and have strong impacts. Survival of the airport business strongly depends on their ability of managing them entirely. Implementation of ERM model can offer an efficient framework for managing these risks. The airport business is a business of managing risks. Any mistake or initiative is a possible source of threat and opportunity in terms of security, safety, quality, environment, efficiency and public health. Thus, airport business risks must be handled efficiently. Furthermore, airports have to create social and economic value for their stakeholders. Therefore, airport management systems must be including implementation of ERM.

A standard best practice model does not exist for ERM implementation in the airport business like other business sector. ERM model is shaped according to the organizational structure and requirements in the Airport Business.

ERM is defined by the Protiviti as an integrated, forward-looking and process-orientated approach to managing all key business risks and opportunities - not just financial ones - with the intent of maximizing value for the enterprise as a whole.

The complexity of ERM precludes "one size fits all" type solutions while the maturity level of enterprise risk management efforts of different companies can vary considerably. "ERM for the insurance industry"; the study by PricewaterhouseCoopers, proved that there is no "one size fits all" solution for designing and implementing an ERM program. At the same time, the ERM process fits all industries, all organizations (public or private, profit or not for profit). But, some strategies and tactics are industry and/or firm specific. In this chapter, best ERM practice surveys, ERM implementation framework guidelines and current practices in the airport business are reviewed briefly since they are detailly presented in the other chapters of this book. The best practice criteria are determined. The chapter helps the best ERM practice approximation since it includes fundamental efforts about this subject.

3. CONCEPTS OF ENTERPRISE RISK MANAGEMENT AND BEST PRACTICE

In the global and volatile air transportation industry and airport business environment, a key source of sustainable competitive advantage and gain of reasonable assurance for achieving of organizational objectives relies on the ERM implementation. The concept of ERM and its importance are discussed below.

No entity operates in a risk-free environment, and ERM does not create such an environment. Rather, ERM enables management to operate more effectively in environments filled with risks. All organizations can benefit from improved ERM procedures in meeting objectives related to strategic direction, operations, reporting and compliance. ERM provides management with enhanced capabilities to align risk appetite and strategy, link growth, risk and return, minimize operational surprises and losses, identify and manage cross-enterprise risks and rationalize capital (PricewaterhouseCoopers, 2006). Recently, there is an increasing attention for ERM implementations in various industries. Many problems appear in an air transportation sector since regarding significant matters of ERM implementations are very limited in both quantity and context. This chapter is prepared to answer this need.

As the dynamics of the market, business environment and changes in regulatory requirements for corporations increase in their complexity, it becomes harder to plot the right course for continued success. Being able to identify and adapt to changes are key success factors for the leaders of tomorrow. In light of these events companies are driven more than ever by the desire to protect their reputation and manage their risks effectively. ERM provides a framework for management to effectively deal with uncertainty and associated risk and opportunity thereby enhancing management's capacity to build value. ERM does not operate in isolation in a corporation, but rather is an enable of the management process. ERM is a part of corporate governance by providing information to the Board and to the Audit Committee on the most significant risks and how they are being managed. It interrelates with performance management by providing risk-adjusted measures. ERM is an integral part of internal control. Given the importance of ERM, the key objectives of this survey were to identify (PriceWaterhouseCoopers, 2006):

1. Current focus areas in corporate risk management

2. Current and planned risk management related functions in the companies.

3. Current and planned risk management processes at the enterprise level

4. Practical next steps to advance ERM within organizations

The organisations reported many benefits of managing risk. The benefits, overall, relate to organizational objectives and the management process. The key benefit is the achievement of organizational objectives. Other reported benefits are better focus on business priorities, strengthening of the planning process and the reliable way to help management identify opportunities. The reported benefits to the management process include: a cultural change that supports open discussion about risks and potentially damaging information; improved financial and operational management by ensuring that risks are adequately considered in the decision-making process; In addition, increased accountability of management (KPMG, 1999).

No risk management process can create a risk-free environment. Rather ERM enables management to operate more effectively in a business environment filled with fluctuating by risks. Enterprise risk management provides enhanced capability to (COSO, 2006):

_ Align risk appetite and strategy: Risk appetite is the degree of risk, on a broad-based level, that a business is willing to willingly take in pursuit of its objectives. Management considers the business's risk appetite first in evaluating strategic alternatives, then in setting boundaries for downside risk.

_ Minimize operational surprises and losses: Businesses have enhanced capability to identify potential risk events, assess risks and establish responses, thereby reducing the occurrence of unpleasant surprises and associated costs or losses.

_ Enhance risk response decisions: ERM provides the rigorous to identify and select among alternative risk responses – risk removal, reduction, transfer or acceptance.

_ Resources: A clear understanding of the risks facing a business can enhance the effective direction and use of management time and the business's resources to manage risk.

_ Identify and manage cross-enterprise risks: Every business faces a myriad of risks affecting different parts of the organisation. The benefits of enterprise risk management are only optimized when an enterprise-wide approach is adopted, integrating the disparate approaches to risk management within a company. Integration has to be effected in three ways: centralized risk reporting, the integration of risk transfer strategies and the integration of risk management into the business processes of a business. Rather than being purely a defensive mechanism, it can be used as a tool to maximize opportunities.

_ Link growth, risk and return: Business's accept risk as part of wealth creation and preservation, and they expect return commensurate with risk. ERM offers an enhanced ability to identify and assess risks and establish acceptable levels of risk relative to potential growth and achievement of objectives.

_ Rationalise capital: More robust information on risk exposure actively provides management to more effectively assess overall capital needs and improve capital allocation.

_ Seize opportunities: The very process of identifying risks can stimulate thinking and generate opportunities as well as threats. Responses need to be developed to seize these opportunities in the same way that responses are basically required to address identified threats to a business. There are three major benefits of ERM: improved business performance, increased organizational effectiveness and better risk reporting.

3.1. Best Practice Concept to ERM and ERM Framework

In order to provide comparability and usefulness to the collection of information regarding "best practices" in risk management, it was necessary to first define "best practice" in the context of this study. This definition was developed jointly with KPMG to be used as well in its international study. "Not all risk management practices are best practices, nor would all good practices have relevance or be readily adaptable to the federal public service. It was concluded that a best practice would be a strategy, approach, method, tool or technique that was particularly effective in gradually assisting an organization achieve its objectives for managing risk. A best practice would also be one that was expected to be of value to other organizations. For example, a practice that was particularly helpful in establishing guidance would be of value to many other organizations, including the Treasury Board of Canada Secretariat (TBS) as the provision of". A best practice is a strategy, approach, method, tool or technique, which was particularly effective in serving an organization achieve its objectives for managing risk. A best practice is also one which is expected to be of value to other organizations.

3.2. Best Practice Framework to Enterprise Risk Management

A best practice framework sets out the areas where best practices would be expected to be of common interest to a variety of organizations. This framework was developed jointly with KPMG to be used as well in its international study. The basic assumption is that a system invests resources in managing its risks, both strategic and operational, in order to achieve anticipated benefits. These benefits, which are often defined as objectives for managing risk could be any combination of:

- Communication for commitment;
- Enhancement of stakeholder value, achievement of corporate objectives;
- Measurement for improved management;
- Support for effective accountability and governance;
- Strengthening of planning and decision processes (synergy, communications, etc.);
- Measurable returns on investments; and,
- Increased confidence of stakeholders.

The authors kept their research of current trends and best practices in ERM with case studies of several organizations: Hydro-Quebec, Bradford & Bingley Building Society, Australian Communications Company, Clarica Life Insurance, KeyCorp, Infineon Technologies AG, Holcim Ltd., and Wal-Mart Stores, Inc. Although these organizations have much in common, ranging from corporate philosophy to corporate structure, the level of success with ERM implementation is varied. Interviews with leading organizations in ERM and literature reviews assisted the authors identify several key success factors for ERM. According to the results of this research, ERM efforts are more successful when there is strong and visible support from senior management and dedicated cross-functional staff to drive ERM implementation and push it into operation. Most executives interviewed implicitly emphasise the importance of linking ERM objectives to the key financial and strategic objectives of the organization and to the business-planning process. In addition, those interviewed suggested introducing ERM as an enhancement to already be entrenched and well-accepted processes, rather than as a new stand-alone procedure, and then proceeding incrementally to avoid great internal resistance.

4. DETERMINING OF BEST PRACTICE CRITERIA TO ENTERPRISE RISK MANAGEMENT

Many books, research and reports published about ERM concept and its conceptual framework. Also, many surveys accomplished about various sectors and industries. But, any study doesn't exist to the air transportation sector and airports. For this reason, this article will assist and support related to newly raising and growing ERM efforts in the airport business across the world. In this study, best practices criteria are determined by these ERM best practice surveys, guidelines, frameworks, case studies and ERM implementation studies are analyzed. They are correctly taken in the 3 main groups. They are;

i. Strategic best practice criteria

- Developing and Establish to ERM vision, mission and strategy
- Integration of ERM into other management practices and management functions
- Creating and Promoting an ERM culture and common language Developing organizational ERM policy and procedures
- Achievement to Corporate Risk Optimization

ii. Operational best practice criteria

- Determining corporate risk appetite and tolerance line; creating corporate risk profile
- Establishing open communication and feedback systems
- Establish ERM information system
- Setting up ERM function and committee
- Setting Up an ERM framework for all aspects of corporate-based risks
- Overall enterprise risk assessment and analysis, enterprise risk mapping and prioritization

iii. Financial best practice criteria

- Use and supply of outsource about ERM
- Supply to Modeling, tools and techniques
- Resource allocation to ERM efforts, requirements and infrastructure
- Establish ERM Framework
- Providing resource to sustainability of the ERM development and continuity

These criteria have qualitative and quantitative characteristic. Selection a best ERM operator in the airport business is considered as the multiple criteria decision-making (MCDM) problem. So, ANP based approach is used in this study. In order to implement the ERM successfully, here raises a critical issue of select best practice criteria of ERM before that ERM implementation. However, although numerous creditable works are devoted to the study of how to build a best ERM practice, few of those have provided methods which can systematically implementation of the ERM strategy and framework. When companies eventually want to achieve best ERM strategy and its implementation, they usually face to consider a large number of complex factors. Typically, the multiple criteria decision-making (MCDM) problem is a decision-making problem basically required to evaluate several alternatives involved in a set of evaluation criteria. Hence, selecting a best ERM operator is a kind of MCDM problem, it is better to employ MCDM methods for reaching an effective problem-solving. Since the ANP has advantages, I develop an effective method based on the ANP to assist companies that need to see of the best ERM practice concepts and its criteria.

5. THE CURRENT ENTERPRISE RISK MANAGEMENT PRACTICES IN AIRPORT BUSINESS: FRAPORT A.G. AND TAV AIRPORT HOLDING CO.

ERM differs from traditional risk management approaches in terms of focus, objective, scope, emphasis and application. It aligns strategy, people, processes, technology and knowledge. The emphasis is on strategy, and the application is enterprise-wide. ERM provides a company with the process it needs to become more anticipatory and effective at evaluating, embracing and managing the uncertainties it faces as it creates sustainable value for stakeholders. It generously serves an organization manage its risks to protect and enhance enterprise value in three ways. First, it serves to establish sustainable competitive advantage. Second, it optimizes the cost of managing risk. Third, it helps management improve business performance. These contributions redefine the value proposition of risk management to a business. One way to strongly consider about the contribution of ERM to the success of a business is taking a value dynamics approach. Just as potential future events can affect the value of tangible physical and financial assets, so also can they affect the value of key intangible assets. This is the essence of what ERM contributes to the organization: the elevation of risk management to a strategic level by broadening the application and focus of the risk management process to all sources of value, not just physical and financial ones (Deloach, 2005).

Commercialization (and in many cases privatization) is becoming a general trend in the airport industry in the sense that airports are increasingly run as commercial business and not as public service organizations. This new scenario has brought opportunities for airport competition and so for further efficiency gains. So, ERM is becoming critical practice in the airport business.

In this section, airport ERM practices reviewed based on TAV and Fraport A.G. cases since they are only current samples related to the ERM implementation to airport business in the across the world.

5.1. Enterprise Risk Management Practice in Fraport AG

Fraport AG Frankfurt Airport Services Worldwide (formerly called Flughafen Frankfurt/Main AG) is a leading player in the global airport industry. Following its initial public offering (IPO) in June 2001, Fraport AG has become the world's second largest listed airport company by revenues. Fraport trades on the Frankfurt stock exchange and has become a member of Germany's M-DAX mid-cap index of blue chip companies. After Deutsche Lufthansa, Fraport ranks as the second largest aviation-related company in Germany. The Financial Times also covers Fraport in its survey of European Top 500 companies.

Fraport's expertise is based on almost 80 years of aviation history at Frankfurt am Main, Germany. Founded in 1924, Südwestdeutsche Luftverkehrs AG – Fraport's forerunner – began operating Frankfurt Airport at the former Rebstock airfield. In 1936, Frankfurt Airport (airport code = FRA) was inaugurated at its present-day location, adjacent to the Frankfurter Kreuz autobahn intersection about 12 kilometers from downtown Frankfurt. A renowned pioneer for decades, FRA serves as Fraport's home base and showcase for the company's know-how and technologies.

Besides managing Frankfurt Airport, Fraport AG and its affiliated businesses provide a wide range of planning, design, operational, commercial and management services around the world. Furthermore, Fraport AG also serves as a neutral partner to the world's major airlines: offering a complete package of aircraft, cargo, passenger and other ground handling services, as well as aviation security services at FRA and elsewhere. The company is also expanding its activities in airport retailing, airport advertising, IT services, e-commerce, intermodal concepts, hub management, and other areas. ICTS Europe, a wholly owned Fraport subsidiary, is now the largest provider of aviation security services throughout Europe.

To strengthen FRA's competitive position in international aviation and to meet future traffic needs, Fraport AG is spearheading the largest development in the airport's history. The €3.3 billion Airport Expansion Program (AEP) includes the construction of a fourth runway for landings and a third passenger terminal with a design capacity of more than 25 million passengers for each year . The new runway will allow FRA's so-called coordinated runway capacity to grow from 80 to 120 aircraft movements per hour – a 50-percent increase. In addition to the AEP, Fraport's is moving ahead with plans for a new maintenance base at FRA for Lufthansa's future fleet of Airbus A380 super jumbos that will be delivered beginning in 2007 (www.fraport.com).

Fraport AG has an extensive risk management system. They are timely determined, evaluate and control the risks with which their activities are related. The primary objective of their risk management system is to ensure a controlled treatment of risk. This gives room to maneuver, enabling risks to be taken if the weighting of opportunities and risks entered into appears to be favorable to the Fraport A.g. As part of their value-oriented management approach, they make their capital expenditure decisions based on this principle. In the Fraport A.G., risk management is integrated in the operating business processes. Management of risks is made by those responsible for the business segments. Risks from group companies are controlled by Fraport AG, partly via the business segments and investment controlling department and partly by representatives of Fraport AG on the relevant supervisory boards. The central body responsible for the risk management system is the risk management committee, made up of representatives from the group's segments. The risk management committee, which reports directly to the executive board of Fraport AG, is responsible for monitoring risks and coordinating measures from the group's point of view. Risk transfer by entering into insurance policies is controlled by their subsidiary, Airport Assekuranz Vermittlungs-GmbH (AAV). Group-wide guidelines require a quarterly documentation and reporting of risk situations. This regular reporting format can be supplemented, on a case-by-case basis, by reporting significant changes. Materiality limits are set for this purpose. The executive board is thus in a position to meet its responsibility for the entire group. The ability of their risk management system to function is checked by their internal auditor department. Their findings serve to continually improve the risk management system. All risks are defined as significant, to the extent they are quantifiable, if their effect on earnings is at least € 10 million before tax, as well as risks which are not quantifiable but could have a similar effect on the net assets, financial position and results of operations. An overall evaluation of the risks to which Fraport AG is exposed revealed that continuation of the company as a going concern is not endangered as far as its net assets and liquidity are concerned and there are no discernible risks endangering continuation of the company as a going concern in the foreseeable future (Fraport A.G., 2006).

Fraport has a comprehensive risk management system. It makes sure that significant risks are identified, monitored constantly and limited to an acceptable level. Fraport actively looks for opportunities and takes them when this is justified by the ratio of the size of the anticipated benefits to the risks involved. Controlled risk exposure is the primary objective of Fraport's risk management system. This objective is the basis for the following risk policy principles:

- The risk strategy is coordinated with the corporate strategy and is required to be consistent with it, as the strategy specifies how strongly the company's operations are exposed to risks.

- Risk management is integrated in the ongoing business process.

- Risks are managed primarily by the organizational units that operate locally.

- The aim of the risk management process is to make sure that significant risks are identified, monitored constantly and limited to an acceptable level.

- Active and open communication of the risks is a major success factor in the risk management system.

- All the employers of Fraport A.G. are expected to participate actively in risk management in their area of responsibility.

Risk management is integrated in the operating business processes. Management of risks is made by those responsible for the business segments. Risks from group companies are controlled by Fraport AG, partly via the business segments and investment controlling department and partly by representatives of Fraport AG on the relevant supervisory boards.

The central body responsible for the risk management system is the risk management committee, made up of representatives from the group's segments. The risk management committee, which reports directly to the executive board of Fraport AG, is responsible for monitoring risks and coordinating measures from the group's point of view. Risk transfer by entering into insurance policies is controlled by our subsidiary, Airport Assekuranz Vermittlungs-GmbH (AAV).

Group-wide guidelines require a quarterly documentation and reporting of risk situations. This regular reporting format can be supplemented, on a case-by-case basis, by reporting significant changes. Materiality limits are set for this purpose. The executive board is thus in a position to meet its responsibility for the entire group.

The ability of Fraport risk management system to function is checked by our internal auditor department. Their findings serve to continually improve the risk management system.

Significant risks

All risks are defined as significant, to the extent they are quantifiable, if their effect on earnings is at least € 10 million before tax, as well as risks which are not quantifiable but could have a similar effect on the net assets, financial position and results of operations.

Economic risks

The state of the economy is critical for the development of passenger and freight movements. The global economy grew by 2.5 percent in 2003, above all in the second half of the year. For the Fraport AG, this means an overall stable situation with no discernible risks, particularly as noticeable signs of a recovery in the economic situation in Europe have improved the overall mood.

Fraport AG is directly affected by the results of crises and armed conflicts leading to the cancellation of routes and flights. Fraport AG is restricted in our ability to counter the risk of a decline in demand. However, as an international hub, Frankfurt Airport can profit from the fact that, in times of crises, airlines tend to concentrate their business on hubs. Hence, in the past the effects of crises could be offsetted after a relatively short period of time.

Market risks

Business with Fraport AG major customer, Lufthansa and Star Alliance partners, made a considerable contribution to revenues in 2003. A deterioration in the relationship with Star Alliance would thus have a significantly disadvantageous effect on Fraport AG. In consequence of the economic importance of Lufthansa and the current consolidation process within the European air transport industry, it can be assumed that, in the long-term, the importance of Lufthansa as a major customer of the Fraport AG will increase.

The financial position of some carriers is difficult. This means that some airlines may possibly have to partly or entirely stop flying in the event of an economic crisis. Any resulting free slots could then be offered to other interested parties, as there is currently no free capacity available. Bad debt risks are being countered as far as possible by active receivables management.

Fraport AG already reported at December 31, 2002 on the risk of a possible restriction of revenues from airport concession fees arising from activities carried out by companies at Frankfurt Airport in accordance with the ordinance on ground services at airports (BADV). As a consequence of the ruling by the European Court of Justice on October 16, 2003, an airport may not demand fees as set out in BADV from a supplier of ground services and other services in addition to charges for using specific airport equipment. A decision in accordance with German law is expected from the upper state court of Frankfurt am Main in 2004. There is a risk that levying airport concession fees will be declared invalid, and the decision may be back-dated. However, the ruling by the European Court of Justice permits a cost-related usage charge. Fraport AG assumes that we will continue to levy fees for ground services in the future. If the fees are lower than currently charged, or if levying fees is no longer possible, this could lead to considerable reductions in revenue.

Risks in Connection with the planned Airport Expansion Program

With the planned capacity expansion via a new landing runway and third passenger terminal, Frankfurt Airport has the opportunity to strengthen and enhance further its status as an international air transportation hub. Frankfurt Airport's expansion is one of the essential prerequisites for Fraport AG to share in the long-term growth in international aviation. No expansion or a significant delay in expansion could mean that air traffic bypasses Frankfurt in the future. Airlines could even transfer some of their flights to the other airports, which would seriously endanger our function as a hub airport. In particular, the transfer of Lufthansa flights or operating units to other airports would have a major negative impact on this airport.

Several interest groups in the region have expressed severe dissatisfaction and resistance to the expansion plans. Interest groups and communities have already engaged the courts regarding the planned airport expansion. Despite the successful end of the regional planning procedure in the summer of 2002, as the first administrative procedure, and the start of the zoning procedure in September 2003, the risk of a substantial delay or legal decision against expansion cannot be excluded. Relating to this, an additional finanical burden could arise. Fraport AG decided to follow the recommendations and results of the mediation procedure which are expressed in the 10-Point Action Program. Fraport AG intention is to reach the best possible understanding with the population and groups affected by airport expansion. The 10-Point Action Program also includes noise mitigation measures in buildings and supports the use of alternative modes of transportation, such as travel by rail. If Fraport AG preferred course of expansion is not implemented, the value of investments already made could be significantly impaired.

Financial risks

Interest and foreign currency risks are initially hedged by setting natural hedge positions, by which amounts or cash inflows and outflows of original financial instruments are offsetting in time and amount. Remaining risks are reduced on a case-by-case business through derivative financial instruments, but these are not used for trading or speculation purposes. Currently, Fraport AG sees no significant interest rate or currency risks.

Legal risks

Manila project

The project in Manila, the capital of the Philippines, to construct and operate an airport terminal was completely written off in the financial statements for the year ended December 31, 2002. Significant current risks and legal disputes in connection with the Manila project are described in the following paragraphs.

During 2003 Fraport AG commenced arbitration proceedings against the Republic of the Philippines at the International Center for the Settlement of Investment Disputes (ICSID) based on the German-Philippines capital expenditure protection treaty. At these arbitration proceedings Fraport is, inter alia, seeking judgement requiring the Philippines Republic to pay damages. The result and duration of the arbitration proceedings are still open. There is a risk that Fraport AG will not, or only partly, achieve the objectives it seeks from the arbitration proceedings.

In a decision on January 21, 2004, the Philippines Supreme Court confirmed its judgment of May 5, 2003 regarding the invalidity of the concession agreements with the project company PIATCO. PIATCO appealed against this further decision of the Supreme Court, and the appeal was rejected on February 26, 2004. During the Supreme Court proceedings on the validity of the concession agreements, in which a decision on the question of damages was not included, the Supreme Court stated that, in the event of a long-term take-over of the terminal by the government, the Philippines government would generally be obliged to pay damages in accordance with the law.

Towards the end of 2003, criminal proceedings were opened against Fraport AG by the Philippines National Bureau of Investigation on suspicion of breach of the so-called "Anti-Dummy Law". The objectives of this law are to limit the influence of non-Philippine persons on certain companies formed in accordance with Philippine law. Fraport AG is of the opinion that its investments in the Philippines were made in accordance with the law. In the event of a negative decision on any possible criminal case brought, Fraport AG's assets in the Philippines could be seized and fines and jail sentences could be imposed on the persons affected.

In 2002 Fraport AG sued PIATCO for repayment of a loan of US-$28 million. As a result, PIATCO in turn sued Fraport AG for payment of PHP1.57 billions (some € 22.5 million) damages and costs. In November 2003, PIATCO and its shareholders agreed to prolong a moratorium regarding the claims by both sides until January 31, 2004, and thereafter on January 5, 2004 the parties unanimously fitted before the court to suspend proceedings for 90 days. Fraport AG intends to attempt to prolong the moratorium.

At the beginning of 2003 the shareholders and directors of PIATCO resolved, against the votes of Fraport AG and the directors of PIATCO appointed by it, to prepare a lawsuit for damages against Fraport AG and their directors on account of allegedly legally improper and damaging behavior. Fraport AG denies these accusations. Furthermore, it is disputable as to whether these resolutions are legally valid.

Furthermore, further investigations have been commenced in the Philippines against current and former members of the boards and employees of Fraport AG, in which Fraport AG is not directly involved or affected as a party, but in connection with which the duration and possible results could have negative effects on, or break up, the settlement negotiations with the Philippine government, or which could question the legality of investments made by Fraport AG in the Philippines or, in the event of a judgement against the persons concerned, could serve as the basis for proceedings to seize Fraport AG's assets in the Philippines. Fraport AG assumes that, with respect to the proceedings against members of management or employees of Fraport AG, the accusations made, to the extent known, have been incorrectly made.

Further legal risks

In a dispute between the new entity owning a partial long-lease agreement for the Sheraton building at Frankfurt Airport and the former owner who sold his rights, Fraport AG could be obliged to make damage compensation payments. The former purchaser now claims the partial long-lease agreement is valueless due to hidden construction deficiencies. Fraport AG believes that the risk that Fraport AG will be obliged to make any payments is extremely remote.

DB Station & Service AG has claimed receivables from services for roofing the railway station from Fraport AG. Fraport AG believes the claims are not valid. We have agreed on arbitration proceedings with DB Station & Service AG. It cannot be excluded that Fraport AG must make further payments for costs incurred in connection with the construction. Furthermore, there is a risk that the investor will not make or delay making the agreed payments due to the postponement in roofing the railway station.

Other risks

Fraport AG business can be negatively affected by events such as accidents, terrorist attacks, fire or technical difficulties. Fraport AG's insurance coverage includes normal risks arising from airport activities and also includes majority-held investments, which are co-insured in Fraport's policies. The insurance coverage includes, in particular, events which lead to the loss or damage of property, including any resulting business interruption costs. Damage claims by third parties arising from operating liability risks of Fraport AG are also covered. As from January 2003, risks in connection with liability claims by third parties resulting from war and terrorist attacks have been covered by the insurance industry up to an amount of US-$1 billion. This also covers those majority-held investments of Fraport AG at home and abroad which are co-insured in the Fraport operating liability policy.

Currently, Fraport AG sees no significant risks in the IT security area.

Risks from investments and projects

Overall political, economic and company specific risks as well as market risks are worthy of mention at certain foreign locations. This applies particularly to Antalya and Lima.

For the modernization and expansion of Jorge Chavez international airport in Lima the shareholders of Lima Airport Partners S.R.L., the concession company, have granted corporate guarantees as collateral for loans, of which Fraport's share is US dollar 10.8 million. If the state of airport operations and the concession company considerably deteriorate compared with budget over the period of the loans, there is a risk that the banks providing finance will take up the guarantee granted by Fraport AG.

The concession to operate the international terminal in Antalya is limited in time to July 31, 2007. A tender offer for a second terminal, which could come into operation in competition to terminal, in order to manage the expected increase in passenger numbers was issued on November 4, 2003 and has meantime been granted to a Turkish company. If the terminal is starting operations before the end of the concession period, this could lead to a loss of revenues at the terminal operated by Fraport AG.

With the typical large number of tender offers in the security services industry, ICTS Europe risks losing some bids and hence losing revenues. In the event of poor performance, there is also a reputational risk of loss of the image and a requirement to pay damages.

There are start-up risks for Tradeport Hong Kong Ltd. and AirIT Inc.. In consequence of an environment negatively affected by the SARS epidemic in Hong Kong in 2003, expected revenues could not be achieved. AirIT operates in the USA in a market for airport-related IT services which has become difficult since September 11, 2001.

Overall evaluation of risk

An overall evaluation of the risks to which Fraport AG is exposed revealed that continuation of the company as a going concern is not endangered as far as its net assets and liquidity are concerned and there are no discernible risks endangering continuation of the company as a going concern in the foreseeable future.

Growing with Security Services

Since the events of September 11, 2001, security measures for international aviation have been considerably intensified again. Increasingly expensive technologies and a growing number of employees are being deployed at airports to monitor passengers, baggage and cargo. These additional security efforts open up considerable growth opportunities for Fraport, which is a leading provider of aviation security services. Through decades of experience in airport security and ongoing technical innovation, the company is solidly positioned in this future-oriented business area.

Internationally, policymakers have been tightening safety regulations. A new European aviation security directive in effect since January 2003 requires 100-percent screening of hold-baggage. This is not an easy task when you consider that more than 48 million passengers used Frankfurt Airport in 2003. Nevertheless, Fraport successfully implemented this procedure at the Group's most important airport. Requirements are continuing to expand not only for passenger controls; since January 2004, employees accessing sensitive zones of the airport must undergo the same security checks as passengers. Security is a key challenge for international air transportation, because today's passenger volume is expected to double over the next 10 to 15 years worldwide.

This growth in volume will only be successfully achieved if security services are provided as an integral part of the total range of services offered at the airport. At Fraport, security has been an integral part of the Group's policy and a highly future-oriented business model for some time now. A strategic milestone was the acquisition of ICTS Europe Holdings B.V., the European-wide market leader for aviation security services.

With 8,600 employees at 46 locations throughout Europe - especially in Germany, England and France - ICTS Europe offers the full spectrum of security-related services. In Germany, ICTS Europe staffs are in action at Frankfurt Airport as well as Hanover, Stuttgart and other airports.

Effectiveness through High-tech

The Fraport gains a practical experience at the Group's Frankfurt operation flow continuously into the development of new security solutions. Technical innovations represent a vital competitive factor - which should guarantee that security requirements are fully met even in the future as passenger traffic increases.

Technologies, which most people have only heard of in science fiction films up to now, are expected to improve further controls in the future. For example, a scanner will check the iris of your eyes - the uniqueness of the human eye generously allows for a reliable check of a person's identity. Already reality today, machine-readable travel documents are being tested in cooperation with Lufthansa and the German Federal Ministry of the Interior. These documents make it possible to check a passenger's identification without physical controls by officials of the German Federal Border Police (BGS) because documents are automatically checked with the BGS's data base. In close cooperation with industry, new equipment is being developed and readied for the market through extensive testing. Among other things, technical innovations should allow for greater differentiation of controls depending on the corresponding degree of danger or risk. Up to now, for example, a passenger who regularly flies the same route is just as intensively checked as someone who is completely unknown. Human and technical resources could be used in a more demand-oriented fashion with individually tailored security measures. The application of new technologies results in more efficient controls, thereby increasing the profit margins in the traditionally labor-intensive security business.

Integrated Security Services save Time

In addition to the technology commitment, intelligent process control makes faster security checks possible, such as for flights to the United States. Before the flight, passengers must undergo a so-called FAA (Federal Aviation Administration) profiling: a special interview before check-in.

For example, Fraport developed a framework that integrates these two measures, thus cutting the waiting time in half for travelers. Shorter controls also useful for Fraport's retail business, because passengers end up having more time for relaxed shopping at the airport before their flight. The ongoing integration of security measures - ranging from check-in to border control and screening of carry-on luggage - continuously reduces the expense for each individual passenger and hence overall costs.

Fraport's so-called Multi Access Control System (MACS) is the world's most efficient and technically advanced gate management and access control system for airports. MACS make it possible to integrate a number of services. It includes all areas of terminal security and combines them with the gate access control system, the flight data information system, as well as alerting systems. By the end of 2004, all the terminal gates at Frankfurt Airport will be equipped with MACS.

Fraport's security services include the areas airport security, airlines and government authorities. Under the mandate of federal government authorities, approximately 1,700 of the Group's employees provide non-uniformed controls. For the airlines, Fraport performs check-in and ticket controls.

The airlines pay the German Federal Ministry of the Interior for security services in the form of an aviation security charge; the amount varies according to the number of passengers transported. An additional 450 Fraport employee is on the job throughout the entire airport site. Their responsibilities include security patrols, monitoring the apron, and controlling access to different areas.

Security for Other Industries

Security as a business model is by no means restricted to the aviation industry. Aviation expertise can be utilized in the ocean shipping industry, where increased controls are anticipated in the form of a corresponding EU directive.

In cargo transportation, it is virtually impossible to unpack each individual container for detailed examination. Thus, intelligent solutions are required here as well. ICTS Europe is undertaking a pilot project in France using snuffer dogs whose keen sense of smell is trained to track down 18 types of explosives - without the need to unpack cargo containers.

Additional revenues are generated by advisory services and training programs in connection with the application of innovative security methods. For example, Fraport's experts support airlines and other airport operators in the application of modern security technologies because increasingly complex technology greater requires expertise on the part of personnel.

5.2. The Enterprise Risk Management Practice in the TAV Airport Holding Co.

TAV Airport Holding Co. is the biggest and pioneer as an airport operator in the Turkey. Furthermore, TAV has many superior and different characteristics from the other airport operators in the Turkey. TAV operates 4 main airports in the Turkey: Istanbul-Atatürk, Ankara-Esenboga, Izmir-Adnan Menderes and Antalya- Gazi Pasa. TAV is operating Gurcistan-Tıflis Airport from February, 2007. Also, TAV is operating the broad geographical field as an operational zone. TAV with its know-how and expertise has been awarded with the construction and B.O.T projects inside and outside of Turkey since 2003. The projects are investment, construction and operation of Ankara Esenboga New Domestic and International Terminal, Izmir Adnan Menderes International Terminal and Tbilisi and Batumi Airports, The Construction of Cairo International Terminal Construction, TB3/Eygpt, Tohid Iranian School Construction/UAE, Emirates New Engineering Centre Hangar Roof Structural Steel Work/UAE, Majestic Tower (G+6P+46) in Al Memzar / Sharjah/UAE, Al Sharaf Shopping Mall Construction, UAE. As the company has grown so fast for the last years, the management has made the decision to gather all the investment, construction and operation activities and facilities in the aviation sector under one roof and for this purpose TAV INVESTMENT HOLDING Co. (TAV Holding) has been established on 1 July 2005 to unite all TAV group companies.

TAV Airports Holding Co. is in a rapidly growth period both Turkey and across the world as an airport operator. Their growth includes service concept and geographical area in both the managerial issues and the operational context. This growth increase and diversify their risks. Also, the growth process is risky. TAV managers are aware of the necessity of providing continuously and strong growth. The process and providing of its continuity are risky. ERM is an unavoidable and important implementation subject for sustainable growth, protection and increase of corporate value, providing to reasonable assurance for organizational objectives, effective and successful airport management to TAV.

TAV has made ERM implementation decision at the end of the 2005 within a formal framework. In 2006, TAV ERM model developed with university-private sector collaboration. Created airport ERM model has been tailored according to the characteristics and needs of TAV airport holding Co. (The model is basically based on: "Kucuk Yilmaz, Ayse., Doctoral Dissertation, Anadolu University, Social Science Institute, Civil Aviation Management Branch, Eskisehir, Turkey, 2007"). New ERM model identified by 32 steps, which is designed as the 6 key components and their sub components:

i. Analysis of Internal environment and Determination of Requirements of ERM

ii. Establishment of ERM Strategy; Establish of Substructure Requirements about ERM

iii. Establishment of ERM Function and Committee

iv. Establishment of ERM Information System and Determination of ERM Framework

v. Establishment of Data Flow and Feedback systems; Analysis of ERM implementation Performance

vi. Providing the continuity of both the ERM system and its development; Restart of ERM process overloops to include new and developing risks and environment.

The implementation of the ERM model is not a "one-size-fits-all" analysis. Therefore, the model is tailored according to the qualifications and various parameters to the TAV Airport Holding Co. All efforts have been achieved with coordinated studies of TAV airport managers as following steps:

- First, TAV Airport Holding Co. is analyzed in respect of ERM infrastructure and capabilities, objectives and demands related to ERM.
- The model is tailored according to the determinations.
- Basic ERM framework and process are prepared according to the general ERM context.
- ERM model is integrated with an organizational ERM process.
- The Airport ERM organization model (AERM-OM) is developed.
- AERM Information Management System (AERM-IMS) is developed.
- AERM information flow system (AERM-IFS) is developed.

TAV has fully AERM concept substructure. ERM is a critical objective for achievement of organizational objectives for TAV executive board and their managers. TAV develops ERM policy, procedures and implementation guide to create a common risk language and ERM terminology. They are considered as following factors in this concept:

1. Fundamental elements: ERM and planning
2. Managerial support and leadership
3. Risk ownership mechanism
4. Set up, risk aggregation and reporting.
5. Assessment, confirmation and follow-up process

TAV has ERM committee. Benefit-cost analysis is correctly counted by TAV ERM committee. According to the TAV ERM philosophy "Every risk does not create value and every risk is not worthy to managing". ERM manages the true risks according to the TAV ERM approach. Critical factors are: value creation and opportunity in the risk. TAV ERM approach leads to the robust management of risks throughout all phases of an enterprise's activities. This result in benefits such as:

- A clear understanding of the risks which could impact the enterprise and how these may be manifested.
- Robust and well implemented systems for managing the risks.
- Employees who integrate risk management into their normal activities.
- Demonstration of risk management performance to stakeholders
- Confidence that the risk profile is understood and being monitored in accordance with the enterprise's risk management plan

The TAV considers that ERM is an integral part of good governance and management practice and is committed to its application at all management levels within a firm-wide framework.

6. APPLICATION OF PROPOSED ANP MODEL TO THE BEST ENTERPRISE RISK MANAGEMENT PRACTICE

The ANP model which is presented in this research has been evaluated in an airport business, which is interested in the implementation of the ERM best practice. The analysis and the implementation of the ANP model are presented in the following six steps. The offered ANP model in the best ERM operator is given in Figure-13.

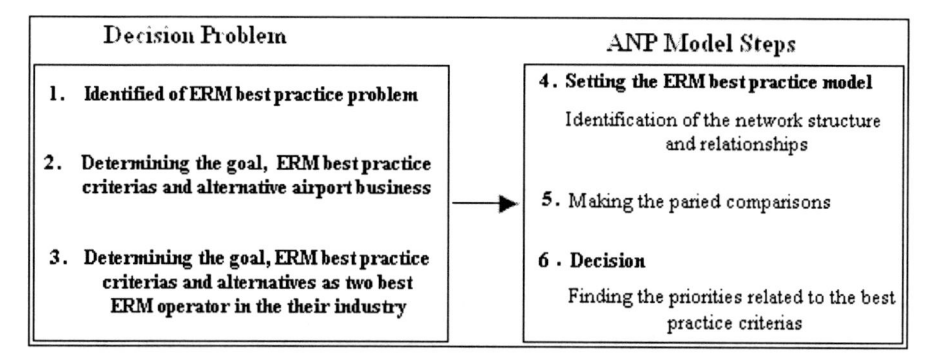

Decision Problem	ANP Model Steps
1. Identified of ERM best practice problem	4. Setting the ERM best practice model Identification of the network structure and relationships
2. Determining the goal, ERM best practice criterias and alternative airport business	5. Making the paried comparisons
3. Determining the goal, ERM best practice criterias and alternatives as two best ERM operator in the their industry	6. Decision Finding the priorities related to the best practice criterias

Figure-13. The proposed ANP model is the selection of the best operator about ERM practice in the airport business.

Step 1. In applying ANP, the first step is to build the model to be evaluated. The overall objective of this ANP model is to evaluate the ultimate relative importance of different factors that impact the best mentation of ERM and assess the best operator to ERM in the airport business. The factors that will be used to evaluate the alternatives are developed and explained in step 2.

In this step, its important components are included in the decision problem. The relevant criteria and alternatives are chosen to be based on the review of literature and discussion with someone both from industry and academia. Also, the first step of the algorithm is the analysis of the best ERM practice problem. The fundamental aim of the best ERM practice problem is selecting the best operator in the airport business that meets the demands or criteria of the best ERM practice. Best ERM practice criteria are determined by the analysis of ERM framework guidelines and best practice survey results. These researches are explained in the literature review section of this study.

Step 2: For the proposed best ERM practice model, overall 16 criteria are determined within the three main critera sets mentioned below:

i) Strategic
ii) Operational and
iii) Financial best practice criteria.

All of the criteria are given in the following table-1. They will be used in the super matrix.

Table-1. The Criteria determination for the best operator of ERM practice by using ANP

THE CRITERIAS TO THE BEST ERM PRACTICE	**STRATEGIC** • Development and Establishment of ERM mission and strategy • Integration of ERM into other management practices and management functions • Creating and Promoting an ERM culture and common language; Development of organizational ERM policy and procedures • Achievement of Corporate Risk Optimization
	OPERATIONAL • Determining corporate risk appetite and tolerance line; creating corporate risk profile • Establishing open communication and feedback systems • Establishing ERM information system • Setting up ERM function and committee • Setting up an ERM framework for all aspects of corporate-based risks • Overall enterprise risk assessment and analysis, enterprise risk mapping and prioritization

	FINANCIAL • Use and supply of outsource about ERM • Supply of modeling tools and techniques • Resource allocation to ERM efforts, requirements and infrastructure • Establishing ERM Framework • Providing resource to sustainability of the ERM development and continuity

Step 3: In this step alternatives are determined as the Fraport A.G. and TAV Airport Holding Co. Selecting the alternatives among the more effective and successful ones in their ERM field of practices by using the preliminary elimination will increase the quality of the decision.

Step 4: Pairwaise comparisons are performed in between the factors. The interactions between cluster sets and elements are determined in this step. The selection of the control hierarchy of the best Enterprise Risk Management Operator Model according to the determined critera is given in figure-14.

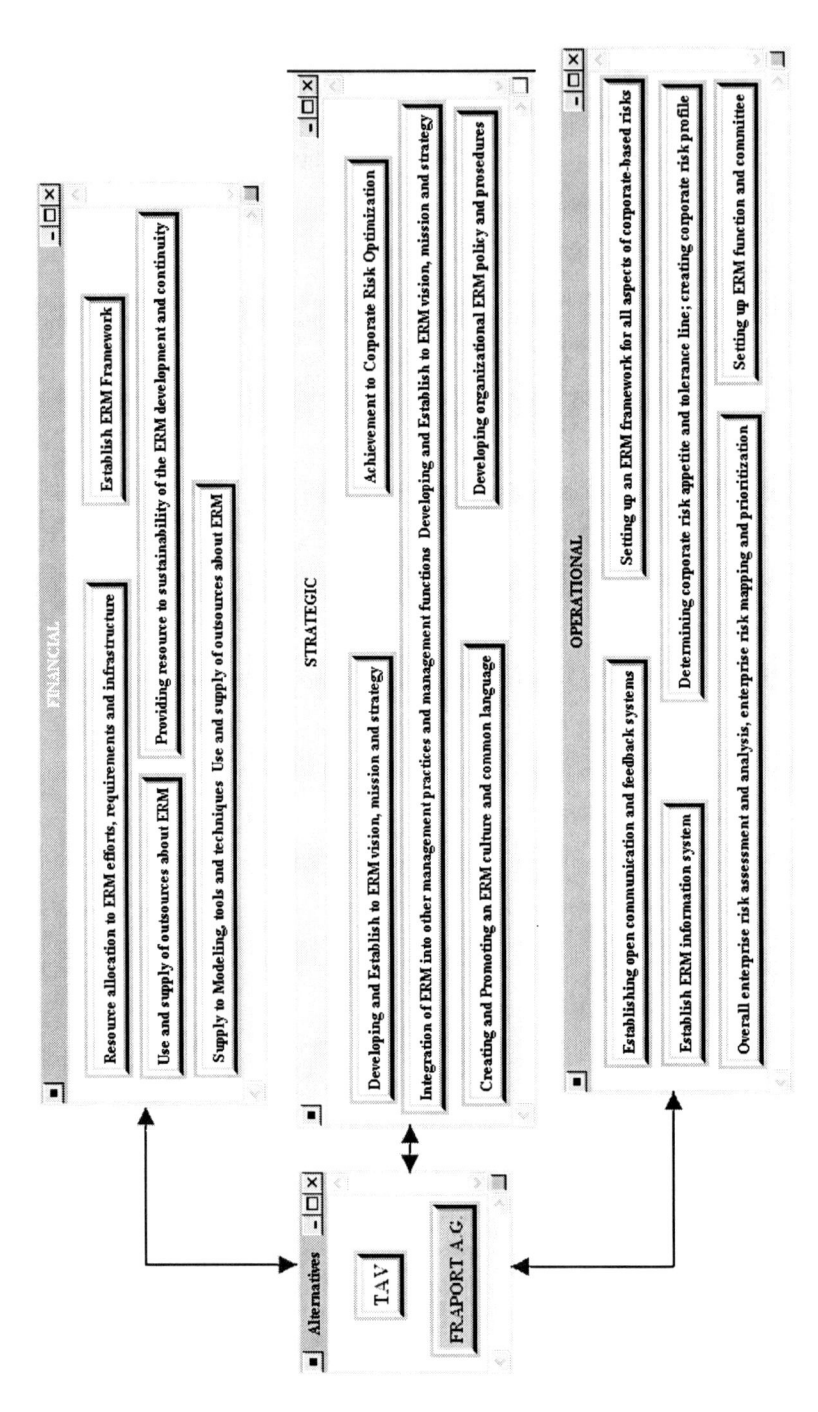

Fig.-14. The ERM best practice network model's control hierarchy (Ayse Kucuk Yilmaz, 2007)

Step 5: Obtaining the overall outcome. Following weighting is obtained by the pairwise. Table-2 shows the priorities of all the factors in the decision-making model.

Table-2. Final reprioritization of alternatives: It is obtained from ANP model.

Graphic	Alternatives	Total	Normal	Ideal	Ranking
	FRAPORT A.G.	0.3449	0.6898	1.0000	1
	TAV	0.1551	0.3102	0.4497	2

The proposed decision model of best operator selection is implemented for 16 criteria under three main criteria sets and two main alternative operators. After this step, I have mine unweighted super matrix. Then priority weights of the sets are calculated by using experts' opinion. Multiplying this priority weight by the unweighted super matrix, I have the weighted supermatrix. The final step is the calculation of the limiting priorities of the weighted supermatrix. According to the final prioritization of alternatives given in Table-2, the Fraport A.G. is the highest priority from the TAV Airport Holding Co. For this reason Fraport is selected as the best operator about ERM implementations.

To sum up, it is hard to decide which is the best practice for ERM certainly since ERM is not a standardized application. Also, ERM is shaped according to the organizational factors. It is mentioned before; ERM is not a "one size fits all" approach. It really is depends on the differences of purposes, the condition of resources and capabilities, and the existing organizational cultures. However, this study shows that; Fraport AG is a best operator according to the current practice. However, they should do many improvements in their ERM system for achievement of best practice. Final prioritization of alternatives and all factors are given in the following Table-3.

Table-3. Final Prioritization of criteria.

Name	Normalized By Cluster	Limiting
FRAPORT A.G.	0.344904	0.68981
TAV	0.155096	0.31019
Establish ERM Framework	0.023149	0.18519
Providing resource to sustainability of the ERM development and continuity	0.026044	0.20835
Resource allocation to ERM efforts, requirements and infrastructure	0.024881	0.19905
Supply to Modeling, tools and techniques	0.024881	0.19905
Use and supply of outsources about ERM	0.026044	0.20835
Determining corporate risk appetite and tolerance line; creating corporate risk profile	0.023501	0.18800
Establish ERM information system	0.019861	0.15889
Establishing open communication and feedback systems	0.022057	0.17645
Overall enterprise risk assessment and analysis, enterprise risk mapping and prioritization	0.019861	0.15889
Setting up an ERM framework for all aspects of corporate-based risks	0.019861	0.15889
Setting up ERM function and committee	0.019861	0.15889
Achievement to Corporate Risk Optimization	0.050000	0.20000
Creating and Promoting an ERM culture and common language	0.050000	0.20000
Developing and Establish to ERM vision, mission and strategy	0.050000	0.20000
Developing organizational ERM policy and procedures	0.050000	0.20000
Integration of ERM into other management practices and management functions	0.050000	0.20000

7. CONCLUSION OF THE CHAPTER

The chapter presents a method for applying ANP in determination of the best operator to ERM implementation in the airport business. By managing risks, managers are more likely to achieve their objectives. Hence, they will be more likely to meet service delivery objectives and targets. Practices such as the organizational philosophy, open communication channels, teams and committees, guidance, and training contribute to a supportive work environment. These practices also support innovation.

The major contribution of this chapter lies in the development of a comprehensive methodology, for the selection of a best ERM operator in the airport business. The chapter also provides a review of the predominant matters, which affects the best practice of ERM. The ANP approach, as a part of this methodology, not only leads to a logical result but also enables the decision-makers to visualize the impact of various criteria in the result. Further, I have demonstrated that the interdependencies among various criteria can be effectively captured using the ANP technique, which has rarely been applied on the context of ERM. The proposed methodology serves as a guideline to the airport managers for ERM implementation-related decisions.

ERM implementation, which is one of the most important managerial approaches of the companies, must be systematically considered from the decision makers. For this reason, ERM implementation is evaluated in a sample ERM framework and guidelines consist of various techniques from the experimental to the analytical ones and its successful applications are performed in numerous sectors. In this chapter, selection of the best ERM operator is considered as a multi criteria decision problem (MCDP) and a simulation is proposed by using ANP. The evaluation criteria are developed according to the best practice surveys and ERM guidelines and the model is applied to the two actual ERM operators in the airport business. This chapter shows that, ANP is a decision tool by making strategically decisions, such as selecting a best ERM operator. Generally, managers may be inclined not to use a sophisticated method, but by using user-friendly software like a super decision, developed by Saaty, the decision making process by using ANP will be handled more easily. Evaluating the operators according to both objective and subjective criteria will provide flexibility to the decision process. Another important finding is that the proposed model reflects the relation how the best practice criteria affect the selected operators more. This chapter takes us one step further to the implementation of ERM as best practice in real airport business.

The effective management largely starts with a proper strategy. Hence, in order to implement the ERM successfully, there exists a critical issue about how companies can better evaluate and select a favorable ERM strategy, framework, and its best practice. However, the best operator selection of ERM usually involves subjective and qualitative judgement. In particular, the best ERM practice is a strategic subject, which is restricted by resource needs, realistic support, time requirements, and conformity with expected outcomes or business purposes. For this reason, the treatment of the best ERM operator selection is required to handle several complex factors in a better objective and logical manner. Thus, the best ERM operator selection is a kind of MCDM problem, and needs MCDM methods to solve it appropriately. Although traditional MCDM methods are based on the independence assumption, the ANP is a relative new MCDM method which can deal with all kinds of dependencies systematically. To assist companies to evaluate and select ERM best practice successfully, I have proposed an effective method based on the ANP. Additionally, this chapter has contributed to extend practical applications of ANP in ERM field. ERM requires to significant managerial efforts and organizational recourses. Both Fraport A.G. and TAV have the best practice criteria for achievement of the best implementation of the ERM.

In this chapter, I have developed a framework based on ANP to identify the degree of impact of factors affecting best ERM practice. I used the ANP to decide the dependence and feedback. ANP is a new methodology that incorporates feedback and interdependent relationships among decision attributes and alternatives. It leads us to a fresh insight about significant matters.

In this chapter, I have determined 16 factors that affect the best ERM practice. The factors affecting the best ERM practice could be qualitative as well as quantitative. There are many qualitative concerns when assessing the factors critical to the ERM practice. ANP enables us to incorporate both quantitative and qualitative factors, which are of the highest importance in selecting the best operator to ERM. This research contributes to both ERM knowledge and ANP implementation. From ERM perspective I propose an ANP-based framework for the selection of the best operator in the airport business related with current ERM implementations. From an ANP implementation point of view, it is the most comprehensive one.

Based on my model, I find that Fraport A.G. is the best operator from the TAV Airport Holding Co. Fraport is given %68 rates about current ERM practice. Most of the existing models that investigate the factors affecting ERM implementation have used various survey methods. I have shown an alternative approach using expert judgment. The ANP approach, as a part of this methodology, not only leads to a logical result but also enables the decision-makers to visualize the impact of various criteria in the result. Since ANP is capable of dealing with all kinds of feedback and dependence when modeling a complex decision environment, I conclude that my results are more accurate. ANP deals with uncertainty and complexity and provides new insights that other, more traditional methods can miss. The ANP approach is capable of taking into consideration both qualitative and quantitative criteria.

Dr. Ayse KUCUK YILMAZ

FINAL REMARKS ABOUT THE BOOK

Risk is a fundamental of being a live, and it is unavoidable in business activity. Enterprise risk management is a reality of airport business. Leading companies and organizations in both the private and public sectors begin to adopt a more systematic, disciplined, holistic, proactive, integrated system of enterprise risk management. Actually, each company, enterprise and each person face with threat and opportunity to a certain extent. Threats and opportunities are the two dimension of the risk concept. ERM deals with managing to the threats and opportunities. This book provides specific information to ERM frameworks and best ERM practice. Also, this book presents a new approach for the best ERM operator selection with ANP based approach.

> Whatever name they put on it - business...holistic...strategic...enterprise - leading organizations around the world are breaking out of the "silo mentality" and taking a comprehensive approach to dealing with all the risks they face.
>
> Tillinghast-Towers Perrin

Enterprise risk management has deserved the attention of management professionals, business managers and academics in the worldwide. Some companies are still organized with the traditional, functionally based and vertically oriented design with little horizontal communications, the so called "silos". Historically, within both private and public organizations, business approaches to risk management have been largely static and silo-based approach. So, risk management has traditionally been segmented and carried out in "silos". This has arisen a number of questions which I experience in solving the problems about the structure of business organizations and the evolution of risk management practice. Traditional risk managers and others assess risks within their own professional field, without looking at the total approach of risks to the business entity as a whole. In recent years, I have seen the emergence of the notion of Enterprise Risk Management as a holistic approach. Partially, it is a response to a sense of inadequacy in using the 'silo-based' approach to risk management. Many major global studies conclude that these silo-based approaches no longer can address the complexity and speed of change in today's environment.

Enterprise Risk Management is placed in the core of the key managerial approaches. Enterprise Risk Management is important for sustainable development and business growth. Organizations need a framework to manage and control significant risks that can interfere with achieving desired results and objectives. This book explains and describes the best practice framework concept for implementing an Enterprise Risk Management. Also, this book gives a best Enterprise Risk Management implementation sample in the air transportation industry. Enterprise Risk Management framework structures and implementation styles are unique to every different airline or airport companies since every company is different from each other. Enterprise Risk Management frameworks are created as company-specifications and characteristics. Related indicators are: corporate strategy, corporate culture, managerial approach and tone, corporate objectives, related industry, corporate risk appetite and tolerances, exposed risks, country, human resources, technical infrastructure capability, complexity of operations and functions, company's size, etc.

Seeking of standard solutions to the Enterprise Risk Management framework and its implementation will purposely create greater risks for the company. Consequently, each company should be tailored to Enterprise Risk Management frameworks according to company characteristics and other related indicators. Enterprise Risk Management should be applied on the air transportation industry: the airline and airport business since Enterprise Risk Management is the fundamental part of the decision-making process and corporate governance. Enterprise Risk Management is an important element of the competition and value creation since Enterprise Risk Management is the fundamental sustainability component.

REFERENCES

Ayse Kucuk Yilmaz. **"ENTERPRISE RISK MANAGEMENT IN THE AIRPORTS: THE MODEL SUGGESTION FOR THE ATATURK AIRPORTS TERMINAL OPERATIONS COMPANY"**, Unpublished Doctoral Dissertation, Anadolu University, Eskisehir, Turkey, 2007.

ABRAMS ET AL. Optimized Enterprise Risk Management, IBM SYSTEMS JOURNAL, VOL 46, NO 2, 2007.

Airport Council International (ACI). Understanding Airport Business, ACI World Headquarters, (2006).

Australian/New Zealand Standard, AS/NZS 4360:2003, (2004) Risk Management.

CAS, Causalty Actuarial Society. Entrprise Risk Management Committee. "Overview of Enterprise Management", Mayıs 2003. www.casact.org/research/erm/overview.pdf, 14/12/2006.

Committee of Sponsoring Organizations of the Treadway Commission (COSO), ERM Framework, September (2004).

COSO, Committee of Sponsoring Organizations of the Treadway Commission. Enterprise Risk Management-Integrated Framework Executive Summary", COSO Publications, 2004, www.coso.org. 21/04/2007.

Crowe Chizek and Company LLC, ERM Point of View, Enterprise Risk Management: A Practical Plan to Get Going Now, www.crowechizek.com, 2006.

DeLoach, James. Enterprise Risk Management: Practical Implementation Ideas, the MIS SuperStrategies Conference, April 26-29, 2005, in Las Vegas, Nevada.

Duncan, Chris. Enterprise Risk: Overview and A Start Up Experience, NC State ERM Roundtable Series, October 2005

Fraport A.G. 2004 Annual Report, www.fraport.de, 14/03/2006.

Fraport A.G. Annual Report 2006, Group Management Report, www.fraport.de, 23/04/ 2007.

http://www.tav.aero/trindex.htm, 25/04/2007.
http://www.finnairgroup.com/investors/investors_9.html, 2007.
http://www.austrianairlines.co.at/eng/Investor/Governance/Risk/, 2007.

Institute of Management Accountants. Enterprise Risk Management: Frameworks, Elements, and Integration, Published by Institute of Management Accountants, www.imanet.org, 2006.

JetBlue Airways, 10-K report. (2003) Annual Meeting of Stockholders.

John Shortreed, John Hicks, Lorraine Craig. **Basic Frameworks for Risk Management, Final Report,** March 28, 2003, prepared to The Ontario Ministry of the Environment.

Kawamoto, Brian. 2001. Issues in Enterprise Risk Management: From Theory to Application. Casualty Actuarial Society Spring Meeting. PriceWaterhouseCoopers Publications, 2007.

KPMG Corporate Finance Comment. "A Snapshot of The Airline Industry", **Turbulent Times,** 2001.

KPMG, Best Practices in Risk Management: Private and Public Sectors Internationally, Ottawa, April 27, 1999, 06-74120/CMC/CC.

Lam, James. James Lam & Associates Inc., *Financial Executive*, January/February 2005:38.

Lufthansa AG, risk management, http://konzern.lufthansa.com/en/html/ueber_uns/balance/oekonomie/risikomanagement/index.html, March 27, 2007

http://www.lufthansa-financials.de/servlet/PB/menu/1016814_12/index.html.

NC State's ERM Roundtable Series, 2005.

O'Toole, Kevin. **Airline Risk,** Airline Business, 04/01/2002.

Pang, David. The Airport Business —Fundamentals and Changing Realities, Contact: A bi-monthly newsletter of the Faculty of Business & Economics, The University of Hong Kong Vol 1, No. 7. Jul (2004).

Performance Management Network Inc., Review of Canadian Best Practices in Risk Management, April 26, 1999, p. 5-6.

Philippe Rochat, Air transport - a global approach to sustainability, http://www.airport-int.com/categories/environment/air-transport-a-global-approach-to-sustainability.asp, 2007.

PricewaterhouseCoopers Inc. **Enterprise Risk Management Methodology, Overview/Baseline**, version 1.2, PricewaterhouseCoopers, 2004.

PricewaterhouseCoopers, PWC, ERM best practices survey, www.pwc.com, 2006.

PWC, FAQs for COSO's Enterprise Risk Management- Integrated Framework, (2007).

Saaty, R.W. (2003). *The* Analytic Network Process: Decision Making with Dependence and Feedback. Retrieved March 16, 2007 from http://www.superdecisions.com/anp_intro.php3.

SAS, **Peyman Mestchian,** Introduction, Journal of Risk Intelligence, Issue 1, 2006, s.2.

Seuamsothabandith, Stacy. "An Examination on Enterprise Risk Management", **Western llinois University Journal**, Western Illinois University Pres, 2004.

Stephen P. D'Arcy. **Enterprise Risk Management,** Journal of Risk Management of Korea, Volume 12, Number 1, May 30, 2001.

Steve Goepfert, Continental Airlines Risk Management Practice, http://www.riskmanagementmagazine.com.au/articles, 18 August 2006.

Steven Minsky, **The Dos and Don'ts of Enterprise Risk Management,** LogicManager Inc. 03/13/2006, http://www.ebizq.net/topics/int_sbp/features/6791.html.

Treasury Board Secretariat, "Best Practices in Risk Management: Private and Public Sectors Internationally", **Final Report.** Ottawa, Ontario: KPMG, 1999.

Wijnen, R. A. A. The Airport Business Suite: A Decision Support System for Airport Strategic Exploration, the American Institute of Aeronautics and Astronautics, Inc., (2003).

www.kpmg.com.tr, 21/04/2007
www.merceroliverwyman.com, 23/07/2006.
Wikipedia, the free encyclopedia, 2007.

Dr. Ayse KUCUK YILMAZ is aircraft maintenance technician in The School of Civil Aviation, Anadolu University in Turkey since 2001. She has master degree of Civil Aviation Management, Social Science Institute, Anadolu University, Turkey 2003. She has doctorate degree of Civil Aviation Management, Social Science Institute, Anadolu University, Turkey 2007. She is working on airport and airline enterprise risk management for 6 years. She has published paper in many important conferences: ATRS (2006 and 2007)), ICRAT (2006) and WCRT (2007). She believes that life is risk management journey. She said that "We should aware of risks in whole life, because risks are present amazing opportunity. We should try to be a risk manager to be successful in the professional life".